How to Win a

How to Win at Roulette

by Norman Squire

OLDCASTLE BOOKS

1992

Oldcastle Books

18 Coleswood Rd

Harpenden,Herts,AL5 1EQ

Copyright 1968 Norman Squire

First published in the United Kingdom by Pelham 1968

Printed and bound in Great Britain by
Cox & Wyman Ltd, Reading

A CIP catalogue record for this book is available from the British Library.

I S B N   1 - 874061 - 03 - 3 pb

Contents

Publisher's note

How to Win at Roulette was first published in 1968 and we have kept faithful to the original text. As such there are several references to the old style Pounds, Shillings & Pence - we trust that this does not lead to any confusion or detract from the value of the information in the book.

Foreword by the Author

Dear Reader,

Originally I called this book 'The Art of Roulette' but my mercenary publishers quashed such aesthetic notions in short order. The eternal fate of the academic when confronted by the commercial is to open his mouth to protest and to have it immediately stuffed with an advance royalty.

Nevertheless the contents of the book are pretty commercial for all that. Artistry comes into it, and must do so if the full value is to be obtained from the arithmetic, but the meat is undoubtedly commercial.

There are plenty of systems from which to choose so selection should be made with care. Please don't grab the first you see and rush to the table intent upon winning a fortune. Systems are weapons to be handled with knowledge and expertise, only obtained after methodical examination and manual experience. So find out what it's all about and have a practise run-through before adventuring. Then you won't get caught on the hop at the table, fiddling around with the wrong number of chips or putting them in the wrong place. That isn't silly, although it may sound so at the moment; plenty of experienced players make mistakes at the table, usually because they have not bothered to get their drill automatic. So get yours right. Then you will have time to incorporate some artistry, get the 'feel' of the table and appreciate when a favourable run is losing its initial impetus and is therefore likely to turn and bite if you carry on at full speed regardless.

At the moment of going to press there is a kefaffle about the legality of the game in Britain. Not to worry. The methods shown in the book are set to conform exactly to the standard conditions of play in continental countries. Any change which may be encountered in this country, made in order to conform to the law, can only be beneficial to you. If a casino is playing 'without a Zero' the odds are immediately in your favour to win. That casino is probably accepting the situation as it stands, accepting the probability of a loss over the year's play in order to keep itself going until the final regulations have been laid down. So the sooner you get there the better, subject always to our previous exhortations about knowledge and expertise. Odds in your favour does not mean an automatic win, any more than the present odds in the casino's favour prevent it from losing quite frequently.

When the standard Rules have been laid down by the Gaming Board to be established under the new Act they will almost certainly be found to be precisely the same as now, and as now operate on the continent. This is a prediction but there is plenty of evidence to support it. If it fails to come true—all the better for you, although there will undoubtedly be far fewer casinos able to stay in business. Even though being on your side however, we cannot hope for this. Things are better as they are. Casinos are fun. They are a new and welcome amenity in this country and may in time supersede many of the traditional clubs. They are the only places where we can have an evening's entertainment and emerge richer than when going in. Poorer no doubt sometimes but even then the amount should be limited by the individual player and can still be less than if he had had his amusement elsewhere.

So—good luck to you, from

NORMAN SQUIRE

The French Roulette Table

The Wheel

On the left of the diagram is the wheel. (La Roue.) It sits in a circular, wooden basin within which it is free to turn. Attached to the centre of the metal wheel is an upright with two crosspieces at the top, making four spokes. A slight pressure upon one of the spokes will cause the wheel to turn. A standard Roulette wheel is a work of fine engineering, and a good heave upon one of the spokes will cause the wheel to turn for fifteen minutes. In play it is not turned quickly, but at quite leisurely speed.

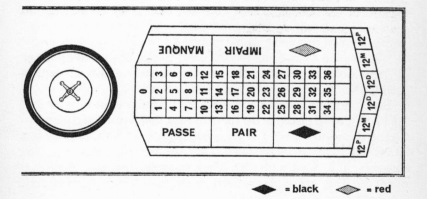

◄► = black   ◄◊► = red

On the rim of the wheel are numbers from 0–36, alternately Red and Black with the exception of the Zero which may be light blue or green. Below each number is a slot formed by metal projections.

An almost weightless ball is flicked round the top of the basin. As it loses impetus, usually after a number of revolutions varying from perhaps eight to fourteen, it drops towards the lower part of the basin; here it encounters one of a number (usually twelve) of diamond-shaped, metal buffers, bounces off at random and then falls to the wheel itself, coming eventually to rest in one of the slots. The number appearing above this slot is the winning number. All played who have backed that number in any one of many ways, win. The amounts they win vary according to the nature of the bets they have made and the size of their stake.

The Diagram

Along the sides of the diagram are six spaces, marked respectively:

Red (Rouge),   Odd (Impair),   Low (Manque),
Black (Noir),   Even (Pair),   High (Passe)

Red and Black are usually shown by coloured, diamond-shaped patches as opposed to the lettering for the others. Odd refers to odd numbers, 1, 3, 5, etc. Even to even numbers, 2, 4, 6, etc. Low and High respectively refer to the numbers 1–18 and 19–36.

In the centre is the diagram of numbers, 1–36. They are arranged in three columns, each of twelve numbers, constituting twelve rows of three. The top row contains the numbers 1, 2 and 3, the second row 4, 5 and 6, and so on. Thus in each column each consecutive number is three units higher than the one immediately above it; and all multiples of three are in the right hand column.

Below each column is a blank space. This refers to its own column and bets may be placed in the space to back that particular column.

Below these—to the right of the given diagram—are six more spaces, stretching right across the table. They are marked from the outside inwards: 12P, 12M and 12D. They comprise two sets of three—identical. They are duplicated merely for the convenience of players, to avoid stretching to place bets.

12P is the première (first) dozen, 1–12; 12M is the moyenne (middle) dozen, 13–24; 12D is the dernière dozen, (last) 25–36.

Standard Bets and Odds

Disregarding the Zero the betting odds are always perfect. Every number is either Black or Red, Odd or Even, High or Low. These are exact even chances so the bank will pay even money.

Disregarding Zero

All even chances	even money
Any dozen	2–1
Two dozens	1–2
Any column	2–1
Two columns	1–2
Single numbers	35–1
Two numbers	17–1
Three numbers	11–1
Four numbers	8–1
Six numbers	5–1

Checking the odds

The perfection of odds may best be checked by stating the favourable and unfavourable positions. Thus, always disregarding the Zero, there are 36 numbers. If we back one number there is one chance for us, 35 against; the bank pays 35–1. If we back two numbers, there are two for us, 34 against; the bank pays 17–1. If we back six numbers there are six for us, 30 against; the bank pays 5–1. If we back a single dozen, we have one dozen for us, two against; the bank pays 2–1. If we back two dozens there are two for us, one against; the bank pays 1–2.

The Zero

For betting purposes the Zero ranks exactly as does any other number. It is backed similarly and pays equal odds.

The Bank's Advantage

With Zero included there are 37 numbers. As the bank pays only 35–1 whereas the true odds are 36–1 it has this small advantage. Against all bets other than even chances this gives the bank an advantage of 2·704%.

En prison (In prison)

When Zero wins all even chance bets are imprisoned. The stakes are placed on the line which borders the outside of their space. If their position loses on the next spin they are naturally lost; if it wins they are *liberated*, i.e. replaced in their original position, freed from prison. The player may now leave them as a fresh bet or remove them as he pleases.

Should Zero win a second time in succession, stakes go into double prison, being placed outside the line instead of upon it. Liberation returns them to the line, and a second win for the position is required to free them completely.

Variations

Different routines prevail at casinos for the en prison positions. Some permit only one degree of prison, some two, some three. Some simply take half the stake and leave the other half in its place, liberated, not using the line at all unless the stake happens to be not divisible by two.

Le Partage (*Sharing*)

A player facing the Zero win, may decide not to let his stake go into prison; he may then concede half to the bank and retrieve the other half.

Thus instead of losing completely when the Zero wins as do the other positions, the even chance bets have a further even chance to be liberated, and, if successful, a further even chance to win. The result is that overall the bank's advantage against the even chances is only half what it is against the other positions, so is: 1·352%.

Overall Bank Percentage Advantage

This cannot be calculated unless the proportion of the stakes actually placed upon even chances and upon the other positions is known. If we consider that an equal amount is staked upon even chances as upon the rest of the diagram the percentage is 2·028.

Disadvantages of the Bank

A comparison with racing is enlightening. A bookmaker may refuse bets at any time; a Roulette bank must accept all bets within its published limits. A bookmaker may close his book at any time; the

Roulette bank cannot do this if the players are there and wish to play. Even at a late hour, when closure of the casino itself is imminent, notice must be given of impending cessation of play. ('Last three spins', 'Last five spins', etc.)

The bookmaker may lay off bets which would otherwise make his book unbalanced. The Roulette bank has no such opportunity.

The bookmaker may, overall, manipulate the odds to suit his own convenience. Thus if two horses are in fact non-separable as far as chance to win goes, but betting upon one of them is disproportionately heavy, the odds for that horse will immediately be reduced to correspond with the weight of money; the Roulette bank pays the same odds no matter how unbalanced the betting may be; it must take its chance of losing heavily on such spins.

The Roulette bank also offers far better odds than does or can any bookmaker. Thus its odds against even chances are permanently 37–36. The bookmaker, confronted with a two-horse race, exactly even form and betting, will demand 5–4 on both horses which is equal not to the Roulette bank's 37–36 but to an almost incredible 45–36.

Should a certain position fail to win for a long time the odds against its appearance are inevitably less. It is almost unknown, for example, for a number to fail to win even once in 300 spins, its average being once in 37, yet, should it fail to win for 299 spins the same 35–1 must be paid on all bets on that number. A player may therefore use a systematic progression of increased bets on it with the practical certainty of winning. This the bank must accept.

Should the first 40 or so spins produce only the top two dozens, it would be strange if the next few spins failed to show a win for the lowest dozen. Again the advantage is seriously with the player.

There are situations where the bank cannot lose, and of which the player—entitled by law to take the bank if he wishes—may take advantage. This is when the possible loss on the highest bet is covered by the mass of smaller bets, when, should the big bet win the bank will break even but, should it lose, the bank will win well. This intrusion by the player must be permitted.

How then does the bank win on balance? It does so by the ancient business practice of small profits and quick returns. A bookmaker may handle a score of races during the day if there are several meetings. The Roulette bank handles hundreds of spins and may handle a thousand.

Placing the Bets

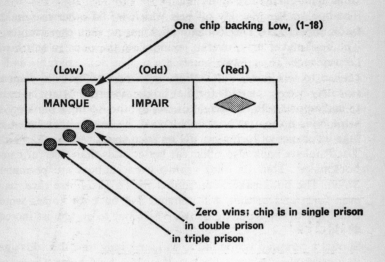

One chip backing Low, (1-18)

(Low)　　　(Odd)　　　(Red)

MANQUE　　IMPAIR

Zero wins; chip is in single prison
in double prison
in triple prison

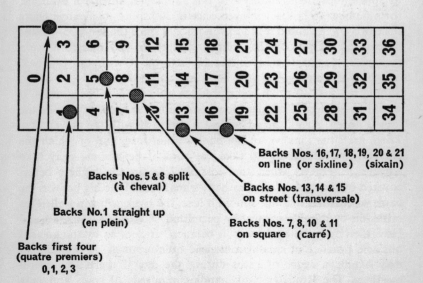

Backs Nos. 16, 17, 18, 19, 20 & 21
on line (or sixline)　(sixain)

Backs Nos. 13, 14 & 15
on street (transversale)

Backs Nos. 7, 8, 10 & 11
on square (carré)

Backs Nos. 5 & 8 split
(à cheval)

Backs No. 1 straight up
(en plein)

Backs first four
(quatre premiers)
0, 1, 2, 3

Note: The limit of degree of prison is automatically the ability of the stake to be halved. If one pound goes into single prison the player may take 10/– and concede 10/– to the bank. If he leaves it and Zero wins again, he may share by taking 5/– and conceding 15/– for now his position requires three consecutive wins in order to win. If he leaves it and Zero wins for the third time he may share, taking 2/6 and conceding 17/6 providing that the minimum stake is not more, i.e. a 5/– minimum would bar this.

Caution: Some casinos allow only one degree of prison, some only two. The player should check, as otherwise the House may take something unjustly. If the minimum is 5/– and only one degree of prison is permitted, two Zeros will take a one pound stake which is legally entitled to be shared, 5/– to the player, 15/– to the bank. In

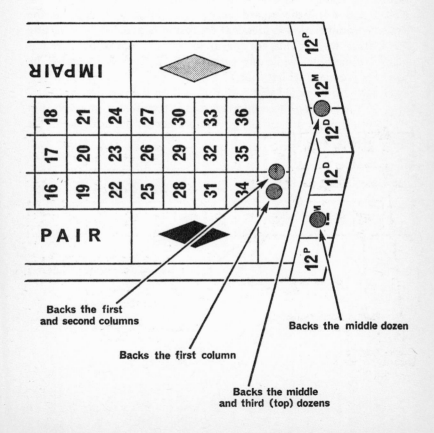

Backs the first
and second columns

Backs the first column

Backs the middle dozen

Backs the middle
and third (top) dozens

such circumstances therefore the player should always share immediately, safeguarding himself against this possibility.

Announcements

The nomenclature of the French table is simple but presents a couple
of curious points which may cause beginners to err. The French
word for 'one' is 'un', a curiously non-descriptive sound which might
mean anything out of explanatory context. It is therefore eschewed
in favour of the French word for 'first', *premier*. Thus if No. 1 wins,
the croupier will announce: 'Premier, Rouge, Impair, Manque.'
(No. 1, Red, Odd, Low.)

Confusion should also be avoided between the split (cheval) on
Nos. 1 and 4 and the square (corner) (carré) on 0, 1, 2, 3. As the
French pronunciation is identical confusion is avoided by inverting
the order of words. Thus the cheval on 1–4 is requested by 'Premier-
quatre' (One-four) while the carré on 0, 1, 2, 3 is requested by
'Quatres premiers'. (First four.)

It should also be noted that a chip placed on the junction of 0, 1, 2
or 0, 2, 3 is backing those numbers and is therefore a transversal at
11–1 even though it does not go straight across the table as do the
other transversals.

0				
1	2	3	3rd. DOZEN	1-18
4	5	6	3rd. DOZEN	1-18
7	8	9	3rd. DOZEN	ODD
10	11	12	3rd. DOZEN	ODD
13	14	15	2nd. DOZEN	◆
16	17	18	2nd. DOZEN	◆
19	20	21	2nd. DOZEN	◆
22	23	24	2nd. DOZEN	◆
25	26	27	1st. DOZEN	EVEN
28	29	30	1st. DOZEN	EVEN
31	32	33	1st. DOZEN	19-36
34	35	36	1st. DOZEN	19-36

◆ = red

◆ = black

The American table

The strict American table as used in Las Vegas has two Zeros. No serious player will therefore play on such a table. In England the American table is modified to include one Zero only and so offer good odds instead of bad.

The diagram has a different layout but the game, the betting and the odds are identical with the French. Play is however about three times as fast. Chips are moved by hand instead of by rake; chips are counted by 'cutting' instead of running out; payments are made by size of stack instead of by being elegantly spread across the table, counted and doubly counted and then pushed slowly forward by rake. The same applies to giving change, an elaborate routine at the French table, a quick transfer by hand at the American table.

The French table manages about 30 spins per hour when busy, 50 per hour when slack. The American table, using standard chips, will average 120 spins per hour even when busy, if fully staffed. This drops to about 90 if no-value chips are used and the services of a cashier are dispensed with.

Bets are placed exactly as on the French table with the exception of the transversal which should always be backed on the 'dozens' side of the diagram; placed on the apron side, chips are liable to be swept up by the dealer when he clears the mass of losing bets.

The language is English although occasional French expressions creep in.

Comparison of language in betting

French	*English*
En plein	Straight up
Cheval	Split(s)
Carré	Corner or square
Transversal	(down the) Street (or 'side')
Sixain	Sixline (line)

French	*English*
Douzaine	Dozen
Premier	First
Moyenne (deuxième)	Middle (second)
Dernière	Third (last; top)
Colonne	Column
Premier quatre	One-four
Quatre premiers	Four first
Trois dernières	Last three
Six premiers	First six
Final	Final
Tiers	Tiers
Voisins	Neighbours
Orphelins	Orphans
Completez	Please complete
Doublez	Please double

Completez

To complete is to place a chip en plein plus one on each carré and each cheval. This is often done when a number has just won. Completion is ordered frequently on a half-completed number, as when a player, having placed, say, No. 17 et chevaux, (five chips) sees it win and asks the croupier to complete the number by adding the four carrés.

Doublez

It is common after a position has won to ask for the stake to be doubled.

Trois dernières

The last three, the transversal 34, 35, 36.

Six premiers

The first six, the sixain 1, 2, 3, 4, 5, 6.

Final

(Often pronounced the French way—feenal—even at an American table.) It designates the final digit of a number. 'Final five' is an instruction to place a stake on each number ending in five, i.e. 5, 15, 25, 35. All Finals from 0 to 6 require four chips; from 7–9 only three. Finals may be à cheval. Final deux-cinq (two-five) is 2–5, 12–15, 22–25, 32–35. Finals à cheval are normally downwards, covering one number and the one immediately below but two numbers in horizontal juxtaposition are valid even though the bet is rare. Final quatre-cinq (four-five) designates the chevaux 4–5, 14–15, 34–35. Three bets only may be placed as the numbers 24 and 25 do not touch. This applies to all horizontals, there being always one pair of numbers not in physical juxtaposition. Any such bet ending in 7–9 will therefore require only two stakes.

Tiers (*du cylindre*) (*Third of the wheel*)

This is a bet on a block of twelve numbers on the wheel, Nos. 27, 13, 36, 11, 30, 8, 23, 10, 5, 24, 16, 33, given in clockwise sequence. Six chips are required and are placed à cheval.

	3	6	9	12	15	18	21	24	27	30	33	36	
0	2	5	8	11	14	17	20	23	26	29	32	35	
	1	4	7	10	13	16	19	22	25	28	31	34	

Le Tiers

Voisins (*Neighbours*)

In the hope that the croupier will fall into a rhythm, dropping the ball into one particular section of the wheel, bets are often placed on a winning (or selected) number and its neighbours, the number of these being specified, but commonly two.

Thus 24 and neighbours, passing five chips to the croupier, causes him to place one chip on each of the numbers 10, 5, 24, 16 and 33, (reading clockwise). To pass three chips would request bets on the three central numbers.

Les Voisins du Zero

A specialised bet on seventeen numbers, in clockwise sequence: Nos. 22, 18, 29, 7, 28, 12, 35, 3, 26, 0, 32, 15, 19, 4, 21, 2, 25. It will be noted that these neighbours are lopsided, nine coming before Zero, seven after. As with the Tiers, the chips are placed à cheval.

Nine chips are needed, and it will be noted that the two last chips are placed on the transversal 0, 2, 3. An alternative, which may be requested, is 'Les Voisins du Zero, Zero en plein', when one of these last chips will be placed on Zero en plein and the other à cheval on Nos. 2 and 3.

Les Orphelins (The Orphans)

Refers to the eight numbers not included in either Le Tiers or Les Voisins du Zero. Reading clockwise they are: Nos. 1, 20, 14, 31, 9, 17, 34, 6.
The bet requires five chips, four à cheval (giving No. 17 a double cheval) and one en plein—No. 1.

It is possible that some American tables, particularly when operating at speed, may not accept these bets—Le Tiers, Les Voisins and Les Orphelins—although the player is of course entitled to place them himself if he so wishes and has time.

Other tables may accept them but place them not upon the actual diagram but upon the rim of the wheel.

A fundamental point about speed difference between the French and the American table is that at the French table the entire drill is performed meticulously and not until every player is ready does the croupier spin the ball. At the American table the ball is spun as soon as all winning bets have been paid. There is no basic waiting upon the convenience of the players. If they do not bet quickly enough they simply have to await the next coup. Or move to a French table.

The Roulette Card

Mises—Reglement—Paiements

A sur 1 numéro en plein	35 fois la mise	
B sur 2 numéros à cheval	17 fois la mise	
C sur 3 numéros en transversale	11 fois la mise	
D sur 4 numéros en carré	8 fois la mise	
E sur 6 numéros à cheval sur 2 transversales	5 fois la mise	
F sur 12 numéros en colonne	2 fois la mise	Plus la mise
G sur 24 numéros à cheval sur 2 colonnes	$\frac{1}{2}$ fois la mise	
H sur 12 numéros, 1 douzaine (P–M–D)	2 fois la mise	
I sur 24 numéros à cheval sur 2 douzaines	$\frac{1}{2}$ fois la mise	
Chances Simples		
Pair, Impair	1 fois la mise	
Rouge, Noir	1 fois la mise	
Manque, Passe	1 fois la mise	

Manque: Numéros 1 à 18. Passe: Numéros 19 à 36
12P: Première douzaine de 1 à 12
12M: Douzaine moyenne de 13 à 24
12D: Dernière douzaine de 25 à 36

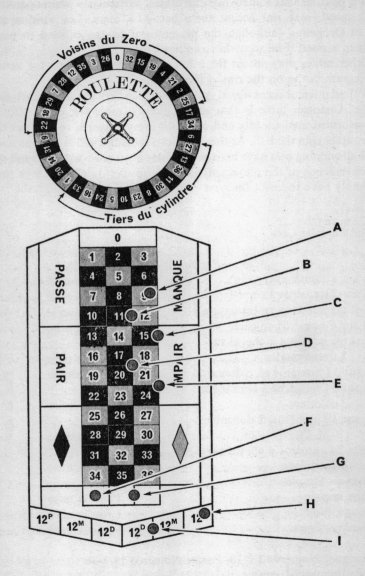

Le Zero n'appartient à aucune colonne ni à aucune douzaine. En sortant if fait perdre toutes les mises des colonnes et douzaines et la moitié de celles des Chances Simples. Il ne paye pas de couleurs.

Aucune mise ne peut être ajoutée, modifiée ou retirée après le 'Rien ne va plus'.

Les 'mises sur paroles' sont rigoureusement interdites.

Le 'Tiers du cylindre' comprend la mise sur 12 numeros du 27 au 33.

Les 'Voisins du Zero' comprennent la mise sur 17 numeros du 22 au 25.

'La Mise' is the stake. Chances Simples are even chances. The effect of Zero has been explained.

Translation

(Aucune mise etc.) No stake may be added, changed or taken back after the 'Rien ne va plus'. (No more bets). Les Mises sur paroles, i.e. announced bets not accompanied by chips—on trust therefore— are strictly forbidden. (All casinos display this notice, but in practice do not adhere to it. Every casino will accept announced bets providing they know the player sufficiently well and have confidence in his ability and willingness to pay if he loses. The announcement to the players of this rule is however necessary for the casino's own protection.)

Definitions

System: a system is a method of selection of target, i.e. the position to be backed at any particular moment.

Staking-plan: this is the manipulation of the amount of stake for each particular bet.

Unit: Bets in the exposition of system are given in terms of units. A unit is the size of stake according to the individual player's needs and available capital.

Minimum: is the minimum chip permitted by the House to be used at the relevant table.

Maximum: this is the maximum amount the House permits to be staked on a particular position.

Progression: an extended series of bets, the stake increasing gradually, the staking-plan manipulated usually so that as soon as a winning bet is made the entire series will show a profit. The simplest form of progression is 'doubling-up'. Progressions however may be less decisive and be compiled so that a win merely cancels one or more losses.

Flat-stake: a system which has no staking-plan other than a single, unvarying unit.

Capital: this is considered to be the amount the player is prepared to lose at a sitting.

Capital-unit ratio: is self descriptive; thus a player playing in units of half-a-crown and possessing a capital—as defined above—of ten pounds, is using an 80–1 capital-unit ratio.

On the table

The Dominant (le gagnant) is the position which has just won. It refers to all even chances essentially but may from time to time be used with reference to dozens, columns etc.

The Non-dominant (le perdant) the position which has just lost. The Deviation (l'écart) is the amount which a particular position moves above or below its average expectation. Thus, in 40 spins the average is 20 for each even chance, (disregarding the Zero). With 30 for one and only 10 for its opposite, there is an advantageous deviation for the former, a disadvantageous one for the latter. The system player should not take it for granted that this sort of deviation will immediately rectify itself by production of a preponderance for the latter position. The extent of any particular deviation is impossible to forecast. Reasonable limits may however be set, and action taken accordingly.

Nomenclature

Calling bets to a croupier is done in abbreviated form. Thus, while a cheval, denoting two numbers, is called, for example, 'Onze-douze', ('Eleven-twelve'), a transversal, three numbers, also uses only two to nominate the position. e.g. 'Sept-neuf', ('Seven-nine'), denotes the three numbers 7, 8, 9. A call of 'Quatre-neuf', ('Four-nine'), denotes the six numbers 4, 5, 6, 7, 8, 9. A call of 'Sept-onze', ('Seven-eleven') denotes the carré of four numbers 7, 8, 10, 11. A glance at the table diagram will show that this is quite satisfactory and not subject to error.

General Advice

Roulette today is almost a national pastime, and will certainly continue to increase in popularity. At one time it was fashionable to be able to play Contract Bridge, a far from easy game. In future to be able to play Roulette will suffice, and this is very easy indeed. It can however be expensive if the right way to play is not known.

The would-be serious player should learn several systems, not merely one, and should familiarise himself with them before adventuring at the actual table. Unless he is simply playing with small amounts purely for amusement—when he can very well win, by the way—he should possess adequate capital. This need not be large. He will find plenty of systems here which demand quite a small capital. But, having it, he must also use it; let it pull its weight. Many bets are only won by weight of money, so to economise on capital which is ready to hand for use is simply to lose the maximum and then, when the opportunity occurs to recoup, to win the minimum.

It is inevitable that a Roulette wheel produce a pattern of numbers. This may remain steady for some time or be continuously changing. The serious player must remain alert to appreciate such change, and be able to accommodate his game to it. Anyone can have a run of luck in a casino, but that is not enough. It enables the player to say that he has beaten the bank, but, wishing to retain that status he must, if he intends to rely purely upon luck, never again in his entire life enter another casino.

This today is deprivation, Casinos offer many amenities and will progressively offer more. To enjoy these, the serious player must be able to hold his own against the bank. And this should not prove an insuperable task. Roulette is a game of skill, and the percentage advantage for the bank is extremely small.

The Roulette table does not win simply because of its percentage advantage. It works on small profits and very quick returns. A bookmaker with a full card may handle 20 races a day; a Roulette table may handle 120 spins an hour.

It often loses. To individual players it often loses heavily, but these losses are usually offset in the main by the losses of other players. Yet with the odds as they are—an average advantage of a mere 2%— it is inevitable that a high proportion of players win. The task of the serious player is to be one of these—consistently. He will lose from time to time of course; nobody can win unfailingly; but on balance there is no reason why he should not be able to beat the table.

He must also know when to stop; be able to recognise when it is 'not his day'. One of the worst faults of many otherwise good players is to have a winning session of say, 50 units but with an outstanding loss-line of eight or nine, and to force themselves into disaster by desperately trying to recover that small amount.

There are two basic types of player—those who go to play, to amuse themselves, who are willing to pay for their entertainment, who expect to lose in the main but are quite satisfied if from time to time they experience the thrill of a big win; and those who go not merely to enjoy themselves but to make a profit also. These are the players who work. The player we shall meet as the 'hard grafter' is their archtype.

Approach to Winning

The player desiring to win at Roulette must approach his task methodically. Were it an easy one casinos would not exist. The would-be winner should not only make careful preparations but, when he does play, consider it rather to be work.

The first essential is to use a sound system. There are many. The arithmetical character of the game lends itself to endless permutation, so that over the years thousands of variations on basic formulae have been employed.

The drawback to every system is that it succeeds for most of the time but produces disaster when it fails. Not only so but, infuriatingly, the sufferer will observe that a different method would have succeeded. It is recommended therefore that a player not use one stock system but several, making his game flexible, capable of accommodating itself to the eternal fluctuations of the wheel.

The second essential is adequate capital. Most money won by casinos is not due to percentage advantage but to the simple fact that the casino possesses more money than does the player and so is not knocked out by the really bad run.

A simple illustration: three men enter a casino. All use a doubling-up method with a line 1 2 4 8 16 32 64. All have equal capital—£32. The House minimum is 5/–. The first man starts with a stake of one pound and loses his entire capital when he encounters an adverse run of five. The second man starts with 10/– but the same adverse run continues to six losses, and he too is knocked out. The third man, starting to play with a unit of 5/–, wins the seventh bet and clears a profit of 5/–. Shortly afterwards he meets an adverse run of seven and joins the other two. The casino, which has seen winning runs for punters of ten or more a dozen times already this evening is playing happily. Little things like that do not knock out casinos. Nevertheless, the third man used his capital more wisely than did the others, making it cover the maximum possible number of bets. But he too is knocked out and may have the mortification of seeing the eighth bet win. His capital was insufficient even though properly employed. The ratio of capital to initial stake is therefore of paramount importance. The higher the capital-unit ratio the better the chance to win.

In these pages we present a variety of systems and staking-plans, carefully constructed and arithmetically sound. The final edifice is there but so are the blueprints, for every serious player should have some knowledge of how a system is constructed. This is merely advice and need not be taken; he may simply select a system he fancies and use it. Nevertheless, human nature being what it is, system players tend to experiment, and this can turn a sound method into something quite disastrous should a knowledge of construction be lacking.

The next essential is self-discipline, an attribute the lack of which is perhaps responsible for more losses than is anything else. The would-be winner must not consider his chips to be money, but must handle them as a bank clerk handles notes—as the everyday tools of his trade. Conversely he must never gamble, never use desperate measures in adversity. And again conversely must never quail before the shadow of disaster, but use his capital to the full; Fortune favours the brave, and to play with frightened money is to surrender all initiative.

The reader will again and again encounter the emphasis we place upon modesty. This may seem ultra-cautious. The experienced player will not think so. So we must be bold yet cautious with our money; consider it not as money but as mere tools and simultaneously conserve it jealously. It sounds far from easy. It is not easy. Were it easy casinos would have gone out of business long ago. But it can be done. All we can do here is to show how.

The Law of Averages

The Law of Averages does not apply to a short session at Roulette. Playing for perhaps three hours at an American-type table, using no-value chips (which is probably the most common situation at a good-sized casino) a player will have to deal with some 300 spins, the number varying from about 260 to 320 according to the number of staff employed, i.e. whether there is merely a dealer or whether a cashier is also present, and how busy the table is.

This gives the Law a fair chance to operate by the end of the session, but it is not normally with the complete session that the player is concerned, but with the immediate play. If he uses a progression which employs his entire capital he is dependent upon the Law of Averages to work accurately the whole time. The moment a serious deviation is encountered his capital is lost and the session cannot be completed. How often then is such a deviation encountered?

Disregarding the Zero effect every even chance position has precisely an even chance to win at every spin. Once it has won it has precisely the same chance to win again. When it has won twice in succession it has again precisely an even chance to win a third time. From this obvious premise we may construct a Table of Frequency of length of losing runs.

TABLE OF FREQUENCY

Bet No.	Loses No. of times. (Series of 100 initial bets.)
1	50
2	25
3	12·5
4	6·25
5	3·125
6	1·5625
7	·78125
8	·390625
9	·1953125
10	·09765625

Bet No. 10 loses ·09765625 times in 100 initial placements, so ·9765625 times in 1,000; giving an expectation of loss of capital once in 1,000 initial placements.

Runs diminish in frequency as they increase in length. Nobody has seen a coin come down heads 1,000 times successively. Everyone has seen it succeed twice. It is therefore reasonable to state that runs of 2 are more frequent than are runs of 1,000. Equally, runs of 3 are more frequent than are runs of 999, and this inequality will continue in diminishing ratio right through the numbers in between.

Nevertheless, to base a system upon one capital loss per 1,000 spins is unwise. Every average contains further averages within itself and is affected by adjacent averages, any one of which may predominate or experience a serious deviation at a precise moment. Runs of ten may therefore come for the most curious reasons, if reason may be admitted here. The casino, playing several thousand spins a day, has an average of such runs to expect, and may fail to show one for some time only to have a rash of them close together. One croupier will say that he has not spun a run of ten for a month; his fellow will have done three in one day. One table may produce such runs in quick succession; another show blank for an extended period. Even a specific chair at a table has an average. Every gambler knows that certain chairs are lucky or otherwise. (Or he thinks he does.) But even that will average out in time. But what time? Coming to the run itself, it also has an average expectation of appearing once per 1,000 spins but contains no guarantee of at which spin. Even should it produce such a run precisely once per 1,000 spins—rationally impossible—it may produce it at Spin No. 1 just as easily as at Spin No. 1,000. Its average may be guessed at Spin No. 500 or 501, but even that is subject to average.

Which average then is going to predominate for one particular session? Who knows? Certainly the punter who relies upon the Law of Averages to win him 999 bets out of each thousand may be said to be unreasonably optimistic. Even if he achieves a perfect average to start with, his losing bet, coming, say, at Spin No. 500, cuts short his profit half-way and makes nonsense of his expectations. The system, arithmetically sound as it might be, immediately becomes a losing method. The next series, (predicating a reserve capital), will be spent not in amassing steady profit but in chasing previous losses.

Obviously, therefore, we must not only have capital in reserve but much more security for the initial capital. We examine this 10-bet sequence financially:

Bet No.	Units staked
1	1
2	2
3	4
4	8
5	16
6	32
7	64
8	128
9	256
10	512
	1,023

This is the eventual loss. But 999 winning bets produce a profit of 999 units. So even if the losing series comes regularly at Bet No. 1,000 we are playing a losing method.

What is more, that losing sequence, subject to the Law of Averages, may easily come two or three times during the whole series of placements. The Law of Averages, by its very nature, is incapable of producing consistency. If it were so capable it would not exist, being replaced—should anyone ever notice its existence—by a Law of Absolute Conformity. The Law of Averages is compiled from a mass of exceptions to an average, some minor, some major, but almost all removed to some degree from the perfect average. Everything will average out at infinity, but will the player live so long? Certainly his money is unlikely to last so long. Obviously therefore, considering method, we must have a longer sequence than one of 10 bets.

The House Maximum

Casinos vary widely in their possibilities for playing complete progressions. This is due to the limits which the House sets for each staking-position. Ten bets is however as much as most will offer. Many provide only nine. Small casinos may give only seven.

Even Chances

Minimum	Maximum	Series										Bets available
2/6	£100	2/6	5/–	10/–	£1	£2	£4	£8	£16	£32	£64	10
2/6	£50	2/6	5/–	10/–	£1	£2	£4	£8	£16	£32		9
1/–	£5	1/–	2/–	4/–	8/–	16/–	32/–	64/–				7

Obviously to play a complete progression at a small casino, as in example No. 3, is foredoomed. Only at the high stake casino are ten bets available. Yet even that is useless, so we must find some method to extend our series. This can only be the use of the Hypothetical Bet.

The Hypothetical Bet

To lengthen the adverse run which is required to beat the progression it is merely necessary to back the non-dominant, the position which has just lost. Black wins. Already then Red has lost once. If we start our progression now, using ten bets, obviously Red will have to lose eleven, not ten times in succession before we are defeated. As Bet No. 11 will—on average—win half the time as well as losing half the time, we have twice as much security for our capital now.

Yet even this is not recommended. If the average loss is now only once in 2,000 spins (mathematically it is not as good as that, but the idea of double security is satisfactory for purposes of illustration) there is still no guarantee that the loss will not occur in the first half of that 2,000 initial placements, and even quite early in that half, once again slashing the profit and turning the method into a loser. Because of this ever present threat of the freak or semi-freak, or even mildly uncommon result, the serious player should not use a complete progression preceded by less than three hypothetical bets, and preferably by four.

Reduction of capital

The player eager to play but lacking capital, willing to take his chance that the disastrous result will restrain its impetuosity for his benefit, may reduce his capital requirements drastically by use of the hypothetical bet.

Thus: a 10-bet sequence, all positive bets, requires a capital of 1,023 units. Retaining the same length of progression but using one hypothetical bet, thus reducing the positive bets to nine, cuts out the final and most expensive bet and so actually halves the capital required.

Capital Requirements

Hypothetical bets	Positive bets	Capital
nil	10	1,023
1	9	511
2	8	255
3	7	127
4	6	63

Thus the complete progression is within the compass of almost any-one prepared to use a 10-bet sequence.

Increase of security

Hypothetical bets	Positive bets	Capital
nil	10	1,023
1	10	1,023

The security for capital is now an 11-bet series and is therefore 'doubled'. With two hypothetical bets it is 'doubled' again and once again with three. A superficial security sixteen times as great may be obtained by using four hypothetical bets plus a series of ten positive bets.

Permutation of this is clearly simple: four hypothetical bets plus nine positive give us a 13-bet series; four plus eight give us a 12-bet series and so on.

It is for the individual player to decide how to balance his capital requirements against his desire for security and to compile the progression most suitable for his needs.

Diminution of profit through paucity of Targets

Once we use hypothetical bets we are no longer betting on every spin of the wheel but may have to wait for a while before the correct number of hypothetical bets becomes available. The beginner, using simple bets, may find this somewhat frustrating at times. The experienced player will be caused no trouble, as we explain shortly in the section on Inherent Even Chances.

Nevertheless, for the beginner at least, the very fact of having to wait must inevitably reduce the rate at which his profit is made. Runs of four may be expected at an American table (using no-value chips and no cashier) perhaps 30 times per hour, giving an expectation of profit—initially—of some 90 units in a three-hour session.

This is attractive of course, yet may be diminished by duplication of targets. Thus Red may lose four times running, giving us a target of Red. But High and Odd may be doing the same thing either simultaneously or with overlap. If we are to back these positions concurrently with our present target of Red, and even one of the progressions goes to the limit, a single capital will not be sufficient. Theoretically we could require a triple capital.

Nevertheless, if security is desired, and it of course most definitely is for the serious player—or he would not be reading this but simply tossing his money on the table for the thrill of the thing—such frustrations must be endured. Soundness of method is essential, and there is no guarantee which player will be lucky or otherwise.

The idea that luck evens out for everyone is utterly fallacious. Luck is also subject to the Law of Averages. It will even itself out if given time. But who has so much time? It may be nice to know that over a period of five hundred years our luck will be just as good as that of the phenomenally lucky player we continually see, but what use is that if we have a bad run for the first hundred years? Luck will even out at infinity. The serious player cannot wait so long. He must safeguard himself as far as is humanly possible against the adverse deviation, and he must do it now, not a couple of light-years hence.

The Insurance Bet

Using the hypothetical bet we have seen that we may either reduce the capital, increase the security or decide upon a balance between these things.

The Insurance Bet enables us to extend the line, using an extra positive bet and so, if desired, one less hypothetical bet—cutting waiting time—but demands a small sacrifice of profit in return.

The double-up series commences: 1 2 4 8 16 32.

Thus if we lose 1 unit in the double-up series our next stake is 2 units, endeavouring to make a profit. An insurance bet here would be a second stake of 1 unit, merely trying to recover the previous loss. Should this also be lost a further insurance bet would be 2 units to recover the previous two losses, and making a line of 1 1 2 instead of 1 2 4.

Comparison of Lines

Double-up:	1	2	4	8	16	32
One insurance bet:	1	1	3	6	12	24
Two insurance bets:	1	1	2	5	10	20
Three insurance bets:	1	1	2	4	9	18

The insurance bets here reduce the capital requirement but the lines still contain the same number of bets, so there is no extra security. A small increase of capital however can produce this.

Double-up:	6 bets	1	2	4	8	16	32		Capital 63
Insurance:	7 bets	1	1	2	4	9	18	36	Capital 71

Profit is sacrificed at Bets 2, 3 and 4 while in return the security for capital is 'doubled'. The principle may be carried further:

7 bets	1	1	2	4	8	17	34	Capital 67

An extra insurance bet at No. 5 reduces the capital slightly.

An even more drastic line falls into a different category:

1 1 2 3 6 10 18 Capital 41. Still 7 bets, but the player deliberately accepts a loss when the line starts to extend uncomfortably. In doing so he departs from the principle of complete progressions which endeavour to clear the entire line with one win.

Here, should he win bet No. 2 or 3 he will simply scrub the line and start again. Should No. 5 win he will cancel three bets, leave the line reading 1 and carry on from there. Should No. 6 win he will again cancel three bets, leave the line 1 2 and stake 3 units to cancel what remains. Should No. 7 win he will cancel the 10, 6 and 2, leaving 1 1 3 and try to cancel two bets by one stake of 4 in order to reduce the line to 1.

This is not playing to avoid making profit, even though it has that appearance; it is playing to reduce the liability whenever the run of results seems to be adverse, husbanding the capital in preparation for when things take a more favourable turn. With Bet No. 7 for example he is trying to win three bets to clear a line of six losses. He is playing not unreasonable Roulette.

He has made no profit if he achieves this but he has taken the absolute minimum of risk. The extremities of approach to the game are 1. the gambler's—to win the maximum while risking losing the maximum; and 2. the hard grafter's—not to lose, and, having succeeded in that, to pick up whatever winnings have accrued on the way. The result of this line is therefore a reduced capital as compared with the double-up method: 41 against 63; extra protection, seven bets against six. The quid for that quo is the sacrifice of immediate profit, reliance for profit being placed upon Bet No. 1. As there must be a good proportion of these which win, all being even chances, the player will inevitably be a steady winner if he can avoid losing his complete line.

The combination of hypothetical bets and insurance bets to produce a line requiring an affordable capital is the task of the individual player and is the basis of his *Staking-plan*. The actual positions he chooses to back and the order in which he backs them make up his *System*.

Combination of Hypothetical and Insurance Bets

An increase of capital, if acceptable, provides 'double' security in exchange for the occasional loss of profit.

Double-up:	1	2	4	8	16	32				Capital 63	6 bets
Combined:	0	0	1	1	3	6	12	24	48	Capital 95	9 bets

This line sacrifices the profit which might be made if the win comes precisely at Bet No. 2. The remaining bets are not affected, all showing 1 unit profit. Security is increased by an extra bet which costs 32 units extra capital and by two extra bets which cost nothing but time.

Frequency of Sacrifice

It should be noted as a point of construction that the Insurance bet at No. 2 costs more than if it came later. No. 1 will win half the time —50%. No. 2 will win a quarter of the time—25%. In 100 initial placements this represents a sacrifice of 25 units of profit.

Had the insurance bet been placed at No. 3 it would have won only one-eighth of the time—12·5%—a definite decrease of sacrifice. What difference does this make to capital requirements?

Double-up:		1	2	4	8	16	32	Capital 63
Insurance at No. 2:		1	1	3	6	12	24	Capital 47
Insurance at No. 3:		1	2	3	7	14	28	Capital 55

Therefore to minimise the sacrifice of profit it is necessary to accept an increase of capital. Balancing one against the other the individual player will decide which method is more suitable to (a) his ambition, and to (b) his pocket.

The principle may be carried further:

Insurance at No. 4:		1	2	4	7	15	30	Capital 59

An extra 4 units of capital is provided. This reduces the sacrifice of profit from 12·5 units to 6·25 units. Reducing the sacrifice to nil brings us directly to the original double-up line.

Having decided upon a suitable line the player will add hypothetical bets. Believing that an adverse run of twelve is unlikely and that an insurance bet at No. 3 is suitable he will use a line:

$$0 \quad 0 \quad 0 \quad 0 \quad 1 \quad 2 \quad 3 \quad 7 \quad 14 \quad 28 \quad 56 \quad 112$$

Plumping for an 11-bet line he merely omits the last bet, reducing his capital requirements by half.

Recommendation

A line 0 0 0 0 1 1 3 6 12 24 48 96 192 is good. It is beaten only by an adverse run of thirteen. It requires a capital of 383 units. (At 2/6—£48.)

Less Capital

The player with minimal capital may reduce the number of bets, taking perhaps a line:

0 0 0 0 1 1 3 6 12 24 48

Panic Stations

The player with a single capital, desperately anxious to preserve it, may adopt a radical approach by saving on the opposite position. He waits for four sleepers and then bets 1 unit. Loses. The next bet should be 2 units, preferable if saving is envisaged. His full positive line will be 1 2 4 8 16 32 64, normal doubling-up. Capital 123 units.

His second and third bets also lose. Fearing disaster he may save with an insurance premium of only 1 unit, by placing a bet of 2 units on the opposite of the position he is backing. Betting on Red, he will place 2 units on Black at the same time as he places his fourth bet, 8 units on Red. (To reduce the stake on Red does not have the same effect.)

The fourth bet loses. His fifth is 16 units, but the 2 units saver on Black has now increased to 4 units. The 16 unit bet loses and he places 32 units, his saver having increased to 8 units. When he places 64 units, his final bet, his saver will have increased to 16 units, and, should his 64 unit bet also lose, destroying his line completely, obliterating his capital, he finds no less than 32 units as a consolation on the other line. This, allied to previous profit, may take the sharpness from the edge of disaster.

Desiring to save more he may concede a loss. The immediate position at the end of Bet No. 2 is that he has lost 3 units. If his line wins, overall he wins 1 unit. This may be sacrificed and a loss of 1 unit accepted by placing a 2 unit saver at Bet No. 3.

Now, if his line wins, he wins 1 unit on the line but loses 2 units on the saver. Basically this means that he shows a profit of 1 unit every time his first bet wins; 1 unit every time his second bet wins; shows a loss of 1 unit when his line wins with any subsequent bet. This is fair enough, for, as every bet is precisely an even chance (disregarding the Zero) he should win two out of every three such bets. Providing absolute disaster is avoided the method is therefore showing a steady profit.

Should disaster arrive and his entire capital be lost he has lost fifteen pounds seven and six, less of course any units he had won before the Hand of Fate descended so heavily, but has saved 64 units, eight pounds, on his saving bet. 'Total' disaster therefore has cost him less than half his capital, an amount he may well have countered before the fatal run came.

Zero

Here is a danger. Zero imprisons the bet and may cause it to be lost. This is not particularly important at an early stage. To illustrate: we back Red. Zero wins at Bet No. 2. Our stake of 2 units is imprisoned. Black now wins and the stake is lost. Zero then has made no difference at all because we always lose when Black wins. If Red wins however our stake is liberated, and the result is that our colour must win twice before a genuine win is established.

A choice of action now faces us. We may continue, leaving the stake where it is, hoping that Red will win again before our line is exhausted. Conversely we may lift the stake and concede a 1 unit loss. A third choice would be to lift the stake and await a situation of five instead of four hypothetical bets, then replacing the stake of 2 units. This gives absolute parity of finance.

The rational action in the event of choosing that way would be to carry on with normal lines of four hypothetical bets for all positions other than the present one. Therefore, having backed a colour, we start any series which offers itself on High, Low, Odd, Even, alternations of four of any of these and double dominants of any of these, but before starting a fresh series on a colour wait for five hypothetical bets.

Zero, however, which arrives when our stake is high is a different matter. It could be expensive if we carry on with the normal sequence, leaving a liberated bet and hoping for a double win. (Again, of course, if the bet loses after being imprisoned we do not suffer technically, because the bet was lost anyway.)

A method of dealing with this, if we decide to leave it, is to place a stake on Zero adequate to recompense us if the entire line goes down. This must, of course, be placed on each successive spin while the line remains in being. This need not be viewed as sacrifice because our bet on Zero can win. It will quite naturally adversely affect our results on many sessions of play, but, overall, Zero should win once in each 37 spins, when we get 35–1 for our money.

On pure average, therefore, we should 'sacrifice' 1 unit over a period for every 37 units we stake on Zero. Certain sessions will show a handsome profit.

Recommended

A line 0 0 0 0 1 2 4 8 16 32 64.

A saver on the opposite colour if the first two bets lose: 2 units. Savers on Zero at Bets Nos. 4, 5, 6 and 7 of 1, 1, 2 and 3 units respectively. (Producing wins, should Zero win, of 35, 35, 70 and 105 units respectively.)

The protection afforded by this is worth study. If Zero wins at Bet No. 6, for example, our stake of 32 units is imprisoned, and so is our saving stake which now amounts to 16 units. A sensible drill is now to share both of them, conceding half to the bank, lifting 24 units. Result: Stakes 1 2 4 8 16 32, + saver 2 = 65 units.

Lifted: 24 units; win on Zero 70 units. Total 94 units.

All danger is now removed; the stakes of 32 and of 64 no longer need to be placed. A fresh series starts with 1 unit.

Drill

If Zero wins, both stakes are imprisoned. Share both.

Bet No. 4 shows an overall profit of 24 units.
Bet No. 5 shows an overall profit of 14 units.
Bet No. 6 shows an overall profit of 29 units.
Bet No. 7 shows an overall profit of 26 units.

The only danger from Zero, therefore, in this series is the somewhat paradoxical one that it may fail to win.

Warning

It must be remembered that even though this method is recommended for the small player, length of line—11 bets overall—is open to serious loss if the player be unlucky. Every additional bet greatly increases security.

Records

If records of results are kept, the Zero in such circumstances should be noted separately. Otherwise the regularity of the record will be disturbed, showing many small decreases and a few sudden and fairly large increases.

Under-insurance in Abbreviated Lines

If the over-riding requirement is conservation of capital we must concentrate upon insurance betting and use a line of minimum length. Three bets are enough for this line and will include two insurance bets. The first line, therefore, is 1 1 2. Having lost this the task is to clear it with the maximum of safety and the minimum of risk to capital.

Speed of clearance and maximum safety are obviously factors which work in direct opposition to each other, so a blend of the two becomes necessary. The stake must be increased in order to clear the lost line as quickly as we may; the factor of insurance must be firmly present in order not to permit the stake to rise too quickly. The second line with normal insurance is therefore 2 2 4.

Under-insurance

Provided that with each winning bet we are clearing more than one losing bet our progress is acceptable, and this need not demand that one winning bet clear two losing ones; it may acceptably clear one losing bet plus a proportion of another. Thus, while a bet of 4 units will clear two losing bets of 2 units each, a bet of 3 units will clear one of them and reduce the other to 1 unit, clearing in practice one and a half losers instead of two. Carried right through a series of abbreviated lines against an adverse deviation this will make a considerable difference to the eventual size of the final stake.

Using under-insurance therefore our first two lines will be 1 1 2 and 2 2 3. Continuing to observe the same principle the following lines produce: 1 1 2; 2 2 3; 3 3 5; 4 4 6; 5 5 7; 6 6 9 and so on. This series has a total capital requirement of 74 units.

Each line has the task of clearing the previous line and no more. Line 6 is there to clear Line 5. When that is done Line 6 is abandoned; Line 5 comes in to clear Line 4 and so on.

e.g. We reach Line 5 attempting to clear Line 4. The first two bets lose, producing 5 5. The next bet of 7 units wins, leaving a residue of 3 in Line 5.

The next stake is 5 units, still using Line 5 to clear its own residue and then to attack Line 4. Should three more bets lose, Line 5 is complete, reading 3 5 5 7 and Line 6 must be brought in to clear it. Should that isolated 3 units residue however be cleared with the first bet of Line 5, 2 units are now spare and may be used to reduce Line 4 from 4 4 6 to 4 4 4. Line 5 remains in operation to clear this. Should two bets now win, reducing Line 4 to an isolated 2, the next stake is at discretion. Line 5 may reasonably be abandoned now and Line 4 used to clear its own residue. Or, playing for maximum safety, a simple insurance bet of 2 units may be employed. If this fails Line 4 still operates as an insurance bet against an outstanding residue of 2 2.

The player must accept the onus for decision with these interior fragments. Only he knows the precise capital available to him and the psychological pressures under which he may be playing.

Inherent Even Chance Positions

The player who dislikes to sit idly for long, waiting for a run of four on Black or Red, may take comfort from the fact that there are ten other even chance positions which he may also use as targets.

The keeping of a record card will inform him when there has been a run of four for Black, Red, Odd, Even, High or Low. But there are other positions:

N	R
	3
29	
	23
29	
22	
	19
35	
	1
	34
10	
33	
	23
8	
	9
24	
6	

There is no run of four for either colour here but the first four give a target of Even. This wins at once, Spin 5, and produces four wins for High, thus giving a target—Low. This wins on the third bet. There is no further chance for one of the standard six, yet other perfectly valid bets are available.

There is now a small wait after Low has won with No. 1. The next three spins produce High Low High which gives us a series of four bets which have gone alternately Low-High. Against this we may validly start a progression, betting that this alternation will not continue. Continuation would produce Low so we bet on High. It wins at once, with No. 23.

Nothing further seems to offer, yet a bet is there; there is a four-time intermittence Red Black Red Black with Nos. 23, 8, 9 and 24. The non-dominant has won four times running, so a genuine bet may be made on the dominant. Continuation of wins for the non-dominant would of course produce Red once more, so our bet goes on Black. If we lose we must transfer to Red, again backing the dominant colour, *not* one particular colour.

What is more there is another position which we have overlooked. This is the double dominant with the numbers 1, 34, 10, 33. Here Red has won twice in succession and this is followed by two successive wins for Black. We may therefore bet that this double dominant will not continue. We must, of course, wait until it has genuinely proclaimed itself, i.e. until the next spin, No. 23 winning, shows that this double dominant on Black really is one and not merely the beginning of a triple.

The bet then will be that the double dominant does not persist. Did it do so, No. 23 being Red, Red would again win. Our bet therefore goes on Black. If we lose that bet, Red winning—and this is the tricky part—we must switch our bet to Red, betting that the present double dominant will not remain one but will turn into a triple.

Validity of Target

B	R
10	
35	
	23
8	
	9
24	

From a run of two or more on Black, the results have gone four times alternately. The valid bet is now to bet that this run will stop. The alternate must not be backed. We back Black, the dominant, the latest winning colour. If we lose, Red wins, so we must now back Red, the latest winning colour.

B	R
	19
35	
	1)
	34)
(10	
(33	
	23

Two opposing doubletons have won. They are in isolation. The first must not be a trebleton; the second must not be backed until it has confirmed that it is a doubleton by the opposing colour having won. (No. 23.)

We are betting that this last result, No. 23, will not become a doubleton, so we must back Black. If it does become a doubleton, Red winning again, we must change to Red, betting that it will not remain a doubleton but will become a triple win.

We note that this double dominant arrived as a valid bet simultaneously with the bet we made on High after the four-time alternation Low High Low High. This may decide us not to back both positions lest our capital be at risk if the wins are long delayed.

Summary, Even Chance Positions available as Targets

Runs of four winners for Black, Red, Odd, Even, High and Low enable us to place bets on their opposites.

The four-time intermittences	BB	R	B	R	B
or	RR	B	R	B	R
or	EE	O	E	O	E
or	OO	E	O	E	O
or	LL	H	L	H	L
or	HH	L	H	L	H

enable us to place bets against a continuation of the non-dominant, the bet being placed always on the dominant.

The double dominants:	B	RR	BB	R
	R	BB	RR	B
	O	EE	OO	E
	E	OO	EE	O
	H	LL	HH	L
	L	HH	LL	H

enable us to place bets against the continuation of doubles, betting, according to the position, that the single win will not turn into a double (back the non-dominant) or that the double win will not remain a double, (back the dominant).

This gives us twelve even chance positions to use as targets. Double dominants however are for experienced players and should not be attempted until the player is completely at home at the table and his routine has become automatic.

Various Systems for Beginners

The beginner at the table, intending to play seriously, requires a drill which is rigid, eminently simple and inexpensive.

Recommended is to wait four hypothetical bets and then stake 1 unit on the opposite, the non-dominant. If it wins, pocket the profit and wait for the next run of four. If it loses replace the stake on the same position. If that wins, the player is all square, will let it go at that and wait for the next run of four. If it loses he tries once more on the same position, still with the same stake—1 unit, and abides by the result.

This method will win almost as often as it loses during a set period, but the player has the opportunity to decide the length of that period for himself. He should decide beforehand how much capital he intends to risk, and should buy chips for that amount at once. A golden rule of Roulette is never to replenish capital. Once a single capital has been lost—finish. The player should also finish when he has won 50% of his initial capital.

A gentle apprenticeship like this will enable the would-be serious player to get accustomed to atmosphere, to learn the ropes, to appreciate what can happen at a table and, by observing the other players, make solid resolutions about how not to play. Once he feels thoroughly at home he may then attempt something more advanced.

Recommended as a second step is the method employed by many regular, small players in continental casinos. This is to use four hypothetical bets once more, but then to back the non-dominant with a progression of three bets 1 2 4 units respectively, stopping of course the moment a win is made, waiting for the next run of four and again betting 1 2 4. A fourth bet in the progression is never made. If all three lose, the loss of 7 units is accepted and recovery attempted with the standard routine.

Choice of table

If there is more than one table in play, it is good policy to go to each in turn and politely request a glance at the record card of a player already there. (This is normal practice in any casino; players always ask to look at other players' cards, so there should be no psychological inhibition.) If the table is showing quick changes it should prove suitable; if runs are long it may be dangerous.

Amending the line

Preservation of capital may be attempted by the use of insurance bets even in this short progression. A line 1 2 3 is good, showing a profit if either of the first two bets wins, finishing all square if the third wins; losing 6 units instead of seven if all lose.
Other lines to be considered are 1 1 2; 1 1 3.

Extra bet

A fourth bet may be used, still preserving capital, with a line 1 1 1 2; 1 1 1 3; 1 1 2 3. The first will accept a loss of 1 unit if No. 3 wins, as will the second. The third is content with equality if No. 3 wins, but may try its luck by using a fourth bet of 1 unit, a sensible investment which is not likely to cost anything.

Letting it Run

Another attractive method is, using any one of these lines, to let the first bet run if it wins. Leave the resultant 2 units there and they may turn into 4 units and be removed to show a 3 unit profit. If they fail to do so, the loss remains at 1 unit and the line may be continued exactly as if the first bet had lost.

Other Simple Methods

Divide the play into short sessions of five spins. By a glance at the record card choose an even chance position which appears to have some preponderance. Stake 1 unit on this position five times in succession. If the result is three wins, 1 unit profit is shown. Start a fresh series of five spins, again checking preponderances. Always back the position which the wheel appears to favour at the moment.

If a loss is shown, write it down. Choose a fresh position and stake 1 unit for the balance of the spins between five and the previous loss, e.g. if the loss is 1 unit, play for four spins; if the loss is 3 units play for two spins. Continue in this manner until the loss is cleared; then start a fresh 'session' of five spins.

Should the loss increase to 5 units, abandon the series in hand, choose a fresh position and use a stake of 2 units for five spins.

If the losses amount to 1 1 1 1 1 2 2 2 2 2 use a stake of 3 units on the next series. Continue to increase the stake each time five losses are shown in the present stake-level, ensuring that each gain is sufficient to clear two losses. Thus a line may eventually appear as:

$$1 \quad 1 \quad 1 \quad 1 \quad 1 \quad 2 \quad 2 \quad 2 \quad 2 \quad 2 \quad 3 \quad 3 \quad 3 \quad 3 \quad 3 \quad 4 \quad 4$$

A series of bets of 4 units have cancelled the series of 1 unit and that of 3 units. A further bet of 4 units has cancelled two losses of 2 units. One more bet of 4 units will now cancel two more losses of 2 units but the line will then read 2 4 4 and will require a bet of 6 units to clear one 4 unit and one 2 unit bet.

As the final bet in such an extended series may tend to become high, the danger that this may occur may be avoided if the previous profit is adequate to stand a write-off of the residue. Thus if the above line eventually shows 4 4 requiring a stake of 8 units, and the previous profit is 20 units, say; it would be good policy to forget the outstanding line, consider the profit to have been merely 12 units, and start afresh.

Alternately, the line may be deliberately reduced to 2 2, equating a sacrifice of 4 units profit, a total of 16 instead of 20 to date and an outstanding line requiring only a 4 unit bet instead of an 8 unit one.

Favourite in five, bet for three

An excellent variation on this provides good practice for the inexperienced player and is not to be sneezed at as a regular system.

The last five spins are scrutinised; the even chance position showing a 3–2 preponderance is selected and backed with a flat stake of 1 unit for three successive spins. The score is written only at the end of the section of play. Thus were there two wins and one loss, in that order, when a normal line (marking wins) would read + + 1, the final figure to be cleared later, with this method the line would either read blank or show a single plus: +.

If there are two losses after one win, the normal line would read + 1 1; this line would read simply 1, each set of three spins being taken as a separate section and the final score recorded as a balance, not as a running commentary.

The selection of target is a 3–2 preponderance normally. Exceptions will arise when there is a 5–0 display when it may be advisable to back the non-dominant rather than the favourite. 4–1 divisions are ignored except when all three positions provide the same; then a choice should be made.

Second target

This will be the favourite (3–2) from the last five spins once again, these five spins being the three which have just been played and the previous two.

Progression

When the line shows a loss of 3 units, i.e. 1 1 1 an increase of stake is made to 2 units. The progression will continue: 1 1 1 2 2 2 3 3 3 4 4 4 6 6 6 8 8 8 requiring, at this level, a capital of 72 units. The player wishing to reduce this may simply increase the basic set of three, as perhaps 1 1 1 1 1 2 2 2 2 2 etc. Here is an example column:

(N)	(R)	
B	R	We hold off for the first five spins. The favourite in these
	27	is Odd.
4		
2		
	27	
	1	
	16	Three bets of 1 unit on Odd produce Nos. 16, 22 and 3,
22		a loss of 1 unit. Line is 1.
	3	
0		Repeat the stake with a target of Low, Nos. 27 to 3
31		favouring that position.
29		
0		
	9	
	23	All three lose, the last because of the Zero. The line

(N)	(R)	
B	R	
	21	becomes 1 1 1 1 and a stake of 2 units is due. The target
	36	is High. No. 21 wins the first bet, reducing the line to 1 1.
	5	The stake reverts to 1 unit, wins one and loses one bet.
	34	Line remains 1 1. Last number was No. 5. The target
	12	remains High. Nos. 34, 12 and 20 reduce the line to 1.
20		Target remains High.
	9	
	23	Nos. 9, 23 and 26 reduce the line to nil. Target remains
26		High.
6		
	30	
	5	Nos. 6, 30 and 5 bring a line of 1. Target may change
11		now to Even. Nos. 11, 7 and 10 make the line 1 1.
	7	Target is Low.
10		
	19	
2		
	9	Nos. 19, 2 and 9 make the line 1. Target remains Low.
	12	
31		
22		Nos. 12, 31 and 22 make the line 1 1. Target is Low.
4		
	34	
	23	Nos. 4, 34 and 23 make the line 1 1 1 and enforce a
26		stake of 2 units. Target High.
	21	Two last spins in column—Nos. 26 and 21 reduce the line
		to 1, stakes being 2 and 1 respectively.

So the series continues, affording plenty of experience at no cost yet with a definite chance for profit. Every player needs experience, and while he may have to pay for it, it is clearly very useful to have to pay the lowest possible amount.

Exegesis

This column will be somewhat disappointing to the pagan reader but it contains a fundamental truth that needs to be appreciated before the true light dawns. It is that the wrong thing may always happen at a Roulette table, catching the unwise virgin very much unaware.

There is no serious preponderance here, so no harm is done either to the player or to the bank. The advantage of this method lies in the fact that when there is one—as frequently there is—the odds are in favour of the player to be going along with it.

It is true that the 3–2 favourability may prevent us from backing a position which actually has a serious predominance, but it also prevents us from backing positions which alternate drastically, creating a situation where we are eternally backing the wrong target. To break even on a couple of columns and then to pocket a nice win on the third is good enough. To win well on two columns only to encounter absolute disaster on the third is no part of our creed. Eternal vigilance is the price of freedom from disaster. When that threatens, it must find us prepared, and prepared to duck out.

The Alembert Method and its Variations

The simple form of Alembert increases the stake after each loss, normally endeavour to win 1 unit of profit when the previous loss is cancelled by a win; and decreases by a similar amount after each win. Thus if we have five consecutive losses followed by five consecutive wins, the line will start: 1 2 3 4 5 and will finish 1̶ 2̶ 3̶ 4̶ 5̶ each cancellation representing 1 unit profit, a bet of 6 units having cancelled the loss of 5, one of 5 units having cancelled the loss of 4 and so on.

In order to make no mistake the record should—initially at least—be written down. At the table in actual play this is often unnecessary. When experience has been gained a surprising amount of arithmetic may be done mentally. Here there is almost none, so a single session at the table engaged in recording should be sufficient for the average player to feel confident in discarding his pen.

Here is a column of a spin record from play:

Backing RED.

(N) B	(R) R	Stake	Line	Units won
	18	1		1 unit won
26		1	1	
6		2	12	
	23	3	1	1
26		2	12	
	12	3	1	1
31		2	12	
	7	3	1	1
26		2	12	
26		3	1 2 3	
	30	4	1 2	1
2		3	1 2 3	
2		4	1 2 3 4	
	21	5	1 2 3	1
	32	4	1 2	1

[Continued Overleaf

Continued from previous page]

Backing RED.

(N) B	(R) R	Stake	Line					Units won
	1	3	1					1
	9	2						1
4		1	1					
	30	2	–					1
15		1	1					
4		2	12					
8		3	1	2	3			
28		4	1	2	3	4		
	30	5	1	2	3			1
	23	4	1	2				1
22		3	1	2	3			
17		4	1	2	3	4		
	36	5	1	2	3			1
29		4	1	2	3	4		
33		5	1	2	3	4	5	
	16	6	1	2	3	4		1
	14	5	1	2	3			1
35		4	1	2	3	4		
	16	5	1	2	3			1
	5	4	1	2				1
6		3	1	2	3			
	21	4	1	2				1

37 spins, no Zero, 18 units won, a line 1 2 remaining to be cleared. It is good play to write this off, accepting 3 units less profit but clearing the line completely. This may make a considerable difference to capital should a long, adverse run be later encountered.

This writing off process may be employed at any time and even partially employed, as, for example here, writing off the 2 units, leaving the 1 unit and starting the line with a bet of 2 units instead of one of 3 units.

A write-off should have been made earlier in this column. When No. 4 wins for the second time, 10 units have been won. The line stands 1 2. Had this been written off then, reducing the profit to 7 units, two spins later the line would have read 1 2 instead of 1 2 3 4. At that precise moment the write-off would actually have shown a direct profit, 7 units won, line outstanding 1 2 = 4 units profit, whereas 10 units won against a line 1 2 3 4 finds the profit completely wiped out.

Of course this 'profit' may not be there for long. If losses are all cleared the write-off represents a genuine sacrifice. But to clear every loss we need to win 50% of spins. This—on average—against the permanent menace of the Zero, cannot be done. Therefore to write off frequently is sound policy. Four such write-offs reduce by eight the number of wins required to clear the line. When a serious adverse preponderance—not necessarily run—prevails, this will make the difference between a line such as 1 2 3 4 5 6 7 8 and one 1 2 3 4 5 6 7 8 9 10 11 12 13 14 15 16.

The difference in capital requirements is obvious enough: 100 units. The difference in psychological pressure seems worth the sacrifice. The outlook of types of player is predictable: the gambler writes off nothing, the hard grafter writes off as often as he can.

Insurance bets may be incorporated into this Alembert series. Instead of the line starting 1 2 3 it may be started 1 1 3 one insurance bet, or 1 1 2, two insurance bets. A large reduction of capital may be obtained by duplication, as in a line 1 1 2 2 3 3 4 4 6 etc. With all such lines the write-off should be made at every opportunity. Units of parity such as these often take a long time to clear. They are attractive because of the reduction of capital, but can be frustrating; a series of alternate losses and wins may leave the player precisely where he started, whereas a staking-plan to give a profit more regularly might have cleared the line entirely. Therefore the more we write off the sooner will the line be cleared.

The same column, backing BLACK

(N) B	(R) R	Stake	Line				Units won
	18	1	1				
26		2	–				1
6		1	–				1
	23	1	1				
26		2	–				1
	12	1	1				
31		2	–				1
	7	1	1				
26		2	–				1
26		1	–				1
	30	1	1				
2		2	–				1
2		1	–				1
	21	1	1				
	32	2	1	2			
	1	3	1	2	3		
	9	4	1	2	3	4	

[Continued Overleaf

Continued from previous page]

The same column, backing BLACK

(N) B	(R) R	Stake	Line			Units won
4		5	1	2	3	1
15		4	1	2		1
4		3	1			1
8		2	–			1
28		1	–			1
	30	1	1			
	23	2	1	2		
22		3	1			
17		2	–			
	36	1				
29		2	–			1
33		1	–			1
	16	1	1			
	14	2	1	2		
35		3	1			1
	16	2	1	2		
	5	3	1	2	3	
6		4	1	2		1
	21	3	1	2	3	

Total 19 units won minus a line of 1 2 3   outstanding.

The Contra-Alembert (Column 1)

This staking-plan increases the stake by 1 unit (or at discretion) after
each win; reduces correspondingly after each loss. We play the same
column again. Backing RED.

(N) B	(R) R	Stake	Line			
	18	1	+			
26		2	2			
6		1	1	2		
	23	1	2			
26		2	2	2		
	12	1	1	2		
31		2	1	2	2	
	7	1	2	2		
26		2	2	2	2	
26		1	1	2	2	2
	30	1	2	2	2	
2		2	2	2	2	2

(N) B	(R) R	Stake	Line
2		1	1 2 2 2 2
	21	1	2 2 2 2
	32	2	2 2 2
	9	3	1 2
	1	4	+ Return to 1 unit.
4		1	1
	30	1	−
15		2	2
4		1	1 2
8		1	1 1 2
28		1	1 1 1 2
	30	1	1 1 2
	23	2	1 1
22		3	1 1 3
17		2	1 1 2 3
	36	1	1 2 3
29		2	1 2 2 3
33		1	1 1 2 2 3
	16	1	1 2 2 3
	14	2	1 2 3
35		3	1 2 3 3
	16	2	1 3 3
	5	3	1 3
6		4	1 3 4
	21	3	1 4

The line shows a loss of 3 units, a gain of 2 units against an outstanding line of 5 units.

This method is always frustrated by the appearance of quick alternations such as appear in the first part of the column. Here a win produces a profit of 1 unit; the stake rises to 2 units, this is lost, the stake reduces to 1 unit which is won and the next stake of 2 units is lost. Equal wins to losses therefore, but a nett loss of 1 unit in each two spins.

This effect is also present when the first and second bets win but the third loses. The first bet wins 1 unit, the second wins 2 units but the third, a loss of 3 units, wipes out the previous two wins.

Success with the Contra-Alembert therefore demands that reasonably long runs should prevail. When that happens and the right choice of target has been made the profit can rise steeply.

How long? We check from the beginning:

A win: 1 unit. A loss: 2 units. Alternations are bad.

Two wins: 3 units. One loss: 3 units. Still bad.

Three wins 1 2 3 = 6 units. One loss 4 units.

Here we show a plus for the first time with a run of three consecutive winners. The profit is 2 units. But an equal amount would have been won, with no risk to capital, by a consistent flat stake of 1 unit. This is therefore not satisfactory.

Four wins 1 2 3 4 = 10 units. One loss, 5 units = +5. A flat stake gains only 3 units, so favourable runs of four are satisfactory in comparison. But again the right target needs to have been chosen, for a second loss will wipe out 4 units of the 5 units profit.

Five wins 1 2 3 4 5 = 15 units. One loss, 6 units = +9. This again will be reduced to 4 units by a second loss. It is clear then that the Contra-Alembert requires runs of five or more to be common.

This would seem to put it out of court for most of the time, yet it has one very great advantage; it is economical of capital. Let the Simple Alembert show a line such as:

1 2 3 4 5 6̸ 6 7 8̸ 8 9̸ 9 10 11 12

the Contra-Alembert line would be:

1 1 1 1 1 1̸ 2 1 1̸ 2 1̸ 2 1 1 1

showing a capital saving of 63 units; 15 against 78.

Follows a Contra-Alembert with a more suitable column.

The Contra-Alembert (Column 2)

Backing BLACK.

(N) B	(R) R	Plus	Minus
	7		1
6		1	
8		2	
15		3	
	34		4
	7		3
33		2	
4		3	
17		4	
	3		5
	14		4

(N) B	(R) R	Plus	Minus
28		3	
28		4	
35		5	
10		6	
31		7	
	3		8
20		7	
11		8	
2		9	
26		10	
31		11	
	25		12
	32		11
31		10	
20		11	
22		12	
33		13	
2		14	
	21		15
	18		14
	30		13
0		imprisoned	
6		liberated	
29		12	

Result: plus 156 units; minus 90 units; balance profit 66 units.

The economy of capital in adversity is well illustrated if instead of backing the right target, Black, the wrong one, Red, has been chosen. The loss on the column is merely 23 units. (9 of them on the last two spins.)

Using this column the Simple Alembert would show a gain of 19 units; 22 units won; line outstanding 1 2. From this we may extract the basic lesson of Roulette: every sound system is a winner at the right time, a loser at the wrong time. Ability to conform is therefore vital. To use one unvarying system the whole time is too dangerous. A knowledge of different methods should be a sine qua non for the serious player. Once this has been acquired he must cultivate his judgment so that he is able to adapt his method to the vagaries of the wheel.

A further point of economy arises when we win at Spin 7 but lose the two following spins. Losing twice our line is 1 2. (Simple Alembert method.) But at Spin 7 we won 3 units against a line 1 2. This should have been used not simply to cancel the 2 in the line, leaving the previous 1 to be cancelled by a later win, but to cancel both bets, clearing the line entirely. This is a continuation of the write-off principle we have already seen. It relinquishes profit but cancels two losses by one win.

The importance of keeping the line short cannot be too strongly emphasised. Providing we keep it short we are *automatically* winning. Let it get out of hand and all previous profit is swiftly wiped out. A bad adverse preponderance will often soar into the twenties. A line ending 16 17 18 is far more comfortable than one ending in 24 25 26. The capital difference is 180 units.

Variations of staking-plan for the Alembert will immediately spring to the mind of the permutation addict. The obvious one is to increase with each win but to drop to 1 unit after each loss.

Like all reasonable methods this is good in the right circumstances. Here it shows a loss of 17 units when backing Red but a profit of 27 units when backing Black. It meets its most common Waterloo in swiftly alternating results, when a series of wins of 1 units is countered persistently by a series of losses of 2 units.

For this column it has been more successful than the Simple, less successful than the Contra-Alembert.

Contra. Alembert:	Win 65	Lose 14
Variation:	27	17
Simple:	16	46

Again it becomes obvious how important it is to be able to change to a different method when the wheel changes. Here the Simple Alembert is at the bottom of the poll, yet we have already seen it do better than the Contra-Alembert.

The Flexible Alembert

The Contra-Alembert has an inherent rigidity in that it frequently hits the floor at a stake of 1 unit and can reduce no more. The Flexible Alembert avoids this by commencing with a standard, higher stake. Common is one of 5 units, so we take that, although the actual number is entirely at the discretion of the player.

Using the same column as previously this method shows a profit of 87 units when backing Black, a loss of 29 units when backing Red.

Ceiling

These figures are achieved with the use of a *ceiling* of 10 units, this being the highest bet permitted. The 'gambler' will naturally use an unlimited ceiling, and for once we have no direct quarrel with him.

Opening bet:		5 units.
After a win:	increase to	6 units, and so on.
After a loss: decrease by 1 unit.		

With an unlimited ceiling the results would have been:

Backing Black:	+97
Backing Red:	—18

Tabulation of Results

Column 1

	Backing	
	Black	Red
Simple Alembert	+16	—46
Contra	+66	—23
Flexible with ceiling	+29	—96
„ unlimited	+29	—150
„ with ceiling, Contra.	+87	—29
„ unlimited, Contra.	+150	—30
Contra variation.	+27	—17

Column 2

Simple Alembert	+14	+12
Contra	—7	—13
Flexible with ceiling	+23	+13
„ unlimited	+23	+13
„ with ceiling, Contra.	—13	—23
„ unlimited, Contra.	—13	—23
Contra variation.	—7	—9

The immediate deduction is that the Simple Alembert is suitable when positions are quickly interchanging. The Contra Alembert does better when one position has a definite preponderance and *when the right target is chosen*. To choose the wrong target will clearly be fatal. The gambler will naturally elect to play flexible Contra unlimited. The hard grafter will probably reserve the Alembert for situations that look extremely favourable, and perhaps eschew Contra altogether.

Alternating the Target

In an attempt to avoid the direct choice of target, a choice which may (a) not matter, (b) be highly successful or (c) be disastrous it is a ploy not without merit to alternate the target at each spin. Thus, should the first stake be placed on Black, the second stake, regardless of result, is placed on Red, the next on Black and so on.

This method has the advantage of avoiding those dangerous long runs for a particular position which can send the stake uncomfortably high and seriously threaten the capital. Yet arithmetic tells us that the alternation is just as likely to produce a long run as is the fixed position. This is avoided to an extent by *missing a spin* whenever three successive losses are encountered.

Sometimes, of course, the wheel will seem to become maliciously sentient, and immediately change its series to accord with the change made by the player. The only remedy in such cases, should the basic method be persevered with, is to attempt to form a pattern which the wheel is unlikely to follow.

As: Playing alternate colours we lose three successive spins. The wheel is going alternately also, but producing the wrong result each time. Miss a spin. The wheel promptly produces a dominant, and then, when we return to our alternation, once again goes against us. If two more successive losers are encountered, the drill should be to play a chosen target for three spins, and, if the wheel promptly switches to the opposite position, retire from the field for a moment. Examine the record with a view to selecting a different target; one of the other even chance positions which is producing results more compatible with our method. If that also goes wrong it is probably not our day, and it is time to retire altogether, remembering, however, that on some days we seem to be unable to go wrong.

The Artificial Random

Many players consider themselves to be unlucky. They may be right. Nevertheless many players who do think this are not really unlucky but the victims of their own obstinacy, often losing heavily through persisting to bet against the wheel when the wheel obviously has a definite preference against them. They choose a target and stick to it far beyond the norm of efficiency.

This type of player may benefit by confining his bets in a straight-jacket prepared for them beforehand. Thus he retains the full 50% of expectation of winning—bar the Zero—while avoiding losing unless the wheel conforms precisely to his pre-set permutation.

Let us say that he backs each standard even chance position in turn. What are the odds against his guessing precisely what the wheel will produce in six successive spins? They are 32–1. So let him produce a set sequence of bets and—again barring the Zero—the odds will be 32–1 that the wheel will not reproduce his sequence.

He therefore constructs an order of bets, for example: Red, High, Odd, Even, Black, Low. He will bet on these positions in this precise order, and the wheel will have to produce the precise opposites each time in order to defeat him.

His sequence for this may be anything to suit his convenience, from a doubling-up, complete Martingale to a doubly under-insured series of abbreviated lines such as: 1 1 2; 2 2 3; 3 3 5; 4 4 6; 5 5 8; 6 6 10, etc.

It would be reasonable, having proved successful with this line for a while, to change his set series, thus giving the wheel a different target. It would be reasonable to select this target from one which has already been produced by the wheel itself, thus eliminating one series which, had he used this target earlier, would have defeated him.

A simplified and quite attractive form of this pre-set arrangement is to back the dominant of the standard even chance positions. We will play a column (from play) using a sequence: Dominant of 1. colour, 2. type, 3. level, and employing the extended under-insuring series of abbreviated lines as above.

Sequence of betting: Dom. Col., dom. type, dom. level.
Lines: 1 1 2; 2 2 3; 3 3 5; 4 4 7; 5 5 8.

(N) B	(R) R	Bet		Line	
17		Bet 1 unit on	Black	Line	
	9	1	Odd	1	
	7	1	Low	1	
2		1	Black	+	
	14	1	Even	1	
	23	2	High	1 1	
26		1	Black	1 1	
	14	1	Even	1	
26		1	High	1	
	1	1	Odd	1	Here a systematic mistake; it happens.
	30	2	High	1 1	
	12	2	Red	1 1 2	
	34	2	Even	1 1 2	
2		1	Low	1 1	
15		1	Black	++	
	18	1	Even	1	
35		2	High	1 1	
	32	1	Red	1 1	
	12	1	Even	+++	
	30	1	High	++++	
	19	1	Red	+++++	
	3	1	Odd	++++++	
6		1	Low	++++++1	
24		2	Black	++++++1 1	
4		1	Even	++++++ 1 1	
	16	1	Low	+++++++	
0		Imprisoned			
	7	Liberated			
6		1	Black	++++++++	
35		1	Odd	+++++++++	
31		1	High	++++++++++	
22		1	Black	+++++++++++	
	18	1	Even	+++++++++++ 1	
	19	2	High	+++++++++++ 1 1	
	34	1	Red	+++++++++++ 1 1	
	16	1	Even	++++++++++++	
	14			++++++++++++++	

A very satisfactory column, even using under-insurance. A plus of
13 units while the series has never reached the third line. This, of
course, will not happen all the time, and it must be realised that once
the series reaches into third and fourth lines, it will naturally and

inevitably take some time to clear, and this may seem—and be—frustrating. Nevertheless, if this type of insurance for the conservation of capital is desired, such sessions must be expected and manfully toiled through.

It is of some interest to the student of systemic construction that, had we backed the exact opposite position, i.e. the non-dominant instead of the dominant, each time, the result would have been a plus of 11 units with an outstanding line of 1 unit.

Against a Repetition of Pattern

The wheel inevitably produces an infinite variety of patterns, and it may be good policy to bet against its producing precisely the same pattern in consecutive series.

The length of the series will be selected by the player. For example, he may decide that the previous six results will not be precisely duplicated in the next six spins. and play a complete Martingale against this possibility. His double-up line will be 1 2 4 8 16 32. He is beaten only if Spins 7–12 produce absolutely identical results to Spins 1–6.

e.g. Spins 1–6 are wins for RRR BB R
His bets are   BBB RR B

Only if the previous pattern is produced in toto is he beaten.

Naturally, the longer the series the less chance that the pattern will be repeated. But against this is the practical difficulty in reading the record card. It looks easy enough but it is not; mistakes in betting will be common unless an extremely precise drill is enforced.

However, taking a far longer series and using a different staking-plan may give us an assurance of non-repetition of pattern, and thus an assurance of success provided that our staking-plan does not over-reach our capital capacity.

The suggested method is therefore a full column for pattern. When one column is completed, bets are made against each successive spin for the next column. This gives a practical guarantee of success with regard to pattern. A double line staking-plan with inclusion of various insurance and under-insuring bets may meet our requirements; 1 1 3 5 5 7; 2 2 5 5 7 9.

We play this against the first three Practice Columns on p. 212.

Having played the first column in some other way, the first bet of the second column is staked against the result of the first bet in the first column. As these positions are in parallel on the record card no trouble in reading them is encountered. The first result in the first column was a win for Black (No. 11), so our first bet is on Red. It loses. The second bet also loses but the third bet of 3 units wins and gives an overall profit of 1 unit.

Play continues in the same way until the Zero is encountered in Col. 1. No bet is made. Play recommences when the next positive result appears.

Should a Zero arrive in our present Col. 2 it is permitted to ride until lost or liberated. If liberated it is permitted to remain if correct, moved to the opposite side if incorrect for its present opposite number in Col. 1.

Thus: stake is liberated to its chosen position Black. The result in Col. 1 for the next spin was a win for Black. The stake is therefore switched to Red.

Playing this Col. 2 against Col. 1 we obtain a result of plus 11 units on the column, but with an outstanding line of 1 1 3 5 which needs to be cleared. Carrying on in similar manner, betting on Col. 3 against the results in Col. 2, we find that this requires some heavy work, but is eventually cleared at the end of the column, giving us the same win of 11 units in two columns play.

It could have given more, but only by the use of a more forceful staking-plan with the accompanying risk to capital.

Staking patterns may, of course, be constructed in any manner pleasing to the whim of the player, producing ideas reaching from the complex to the bizarre. One fan of the late Sir W. Churchill uses that name—in full—Winston Spencer Churchill which produces O E E-R H R L L. He starts this sequence normally but when it is finished plays it backwards. Having done that he rotates it. It has been played once starting with Odd and once starting with Low. He now starts with the second letter, Even. Having completed that, with the third, another Even, then the fourth, Red, and so on. He never backs Black directly although naturally plenty of his wins coincide with Black winning.

The continuous change of pattern is an attempt to prevent the wheel from producing a pattern in obverse. The cynic might say that it is an attempt to find a pattern that the wheel will match.

Write-off Columns

The Write-off is of such importance that an extended examination of it should be made. Following are six columns from play. They are not of standard, 37-spin length but are of 31. This happens simply because the casino at which they were played provides cards with only 31 spaces. They are from an American table, no cashier, no-value chips, and an average spinning time of 90 spins per hour. They thus represent almost exactly two hours play. (No-value chips are chips with no denomination marked upon them; each set is of a different colour so that only the player who is actually using them can retrieve the winnings; and each player informs the dealer of the amount he wishes the single chip to represent. Thus at this particular table, with a maximum of £200 and a minimum of 5/- players were using them at values varying from 5/- to £5. A marker placed upon the rim of the wheel confirms the value set upon each particular colour.)

		SIMPLE ALEMBERT	
Backing BLACK		Initial stake 1 unit	No starting line
(N)	(R)		
B	R	No write-off	Write-off
	30	1	1
	34	1 2	1 2
24		1 2	
	21	1 2	1
10		1 2	1
15		1	+
22		+	+
	34	1	1
28		1	1
25		+	+
	1	1	1
6		1	1
25		+	+
	34	1	1
33		1	1
33		+	+

[Continued Overleaf

Continued from previous page]

Backing BLACK		Initial stake 1 unit	No starting line
(N)	(R)		
B	R	No write-off	Write-off
22		+	+
15		+	+
	32	1	1
17		~~1~~	~~1~~
20		+	+
	19	1	1
	18	1 2	1 2
24		1 ~~2~~	
	0	imprisoned	imprisoned
26		liberated	liberated
8		+	
	34	1	1
33		~~1~~	~~1~~
20		+	+
	19	1	1

Each figure crossed off represents a gain of 1 unit as does each +
symbol. In the first line no write-off has been made. In the second line
the write-off has been made whenever possible.

Result:
Line 1. + 18 units, 1 unit outstanding to be cleared.
Line 2. + 15 units, 1 unit outstanding to be cleared.

The writing-off principle has therefore cost an insurance premium of
3 units.

Backing BLACK. Line starts: 1.

(N)	(R)		
B	R	No write-off	Write-off
11		~~1~~	~~1~~
	5	1	1
	12	1 2	1 2
20		1 ~~2~~	
	36	1 2	1
26		1 ~~2~~	~~1~~
	3	1 2	1
	18	1 2 3	1 2
2		1 2 ~~3~~	
	34	1 2 3	1
11		1 2 ~~3~~	~~1~~
4		1 ~~2~~	+
6		~~1~~	+
	3	1	1

Backing **BLACK**. Line starts: 1.

(N) B	(R) R	No write-off	Write-off
35		~~1~~	~~1~~
	0	imprisoned	imprisoned
	21	1	1
35		~~1~~	~~1~~
4		+	+
	21	1	1
35		~~1~~	~~1~~
4		+	+
	21	1	1
4		~~1~~	~~1~~
8		+	+
6		+	+
17		+	+
	32	1	1
6		~~1~~	~~1~~
	20	1	1
	12	1 2	1 2
	18	1 2 3	1 2 3
35		1 2 ~~3~~	1 2 ~~3~~
26		1 ~~2~~	

Result:

Line 1. + 19 units. Line of 1 unit outstanding.
Line 2. + 16 units. Line cleared.

Running total: No write-off: + 37. 1 to clear.
Write-off: + 31.

Backing **BLACK**. Line 1 starts 1. Line 2 starts clear.

(N) B	(R) R	No write-off	Write-off
	34	1 2	1
22		1 ~~2~~	~~1~~
	16	1 2	1
	23	1 2 3	1 2
13		1 2 ~~3~~	
11		1 ~~2~~	+
	18	1 2	1
11		1 ~~2~~	~~1~~
15		~~1~~	+
20		+	+
	23	1	1

[Continued Overleaf

Continued from previous page]

Backing BLACK. Line 1 starts 1. Line 2 starts clear.

(N) B	(R) R	No write-off	Write-off
31		~~1~~	~~1~~
	5	1	1
	1	1 2	1 2
13		1 ~~2~~	
8		~~1~~	+
	12	1	1
	1	1 2	1 2
	3	1 2 3	1 2 3
	30	1 2 3 4	1 2 3 4
	36	1 2 3 4 5	1 2 3 4 5
	18	1 2 3 4 5 6	1 2 3 4 5 6
29		1 2 3 4 5 ~~6~~	1 2 3 4 5 ~~6~~
	21	1 2 3 4 5 6	1 2 3 4 5 6
13		1 2 3 4 5 ~~6~~	1 2 3 4 5 ~~6~~
	3	1 2 3 4 5 6	1 2 3 4 5 6
20		1 2 3 4 5 ~~6~~	1 2 3 4 5 ~~6~~
29		1 2 3 4 ~~5~~	1 2 3 4 ~~5~~
15		1 2 3 ~~4~~	1 2 3 ~~4~~
35		1 2 ~~3~~	1 2 ~~3~~
	5	1 2 3	1 2 3

Results:

Line 1. + 15. Outstanding: 6 units.
Line 2. + 13. Outstanding: 6 units.

Running totals: No write-off: + 52. 1 2 3 to clear.
Write-off: + 44. 1 2 3 to clear.

Backing BLACK. Both lines start 1 2 3.

(N) B	(R) R	No write-off	Write-off
	34	1 2 3 4	1 2 3 4
	18	1 2 3 4 5	1 2 3 4 5
29		1 2 3 4 ~~5~~	1 2 3 4 ~~5~~
	36	1 2 3 4 5	1 2 3 4 5
33		1 2 3 4 ~~5~~	1 2 3 4 ~~5~~
35		1 2 3 ~~4~~	1 2 3 ~~4~~
8		1 2 ~~3~~	1 2 ~~3~~
24		1 ~~2~~	
	21	1 2	1
	23	1 2 3	1 2
	12	1 2 3 4	1 2 3
	30	1 2 3 4 5	1 2 3 4

Backing BLACK. Both lines start 1 2 3.

(N) B	(R) R	No write-off	Write-off
28		1 2 3 4 ~~5~~	1 2 3 ~~4~~
17		1 2 3 ~~4~~	1 2 ~~3~~
	34	1 2 3 4	1 2 3
	3	1 2 3 4 5	1 2 3 4
22		1 2 3 4 ~~5~~	1 2 3 ~~4~~
4		1 2 3 ~~4~~	1 2 ~~3~~
6		1 2 ~~3~~	
	25	1 2 3	1
15		1 2 ~~3~~	~~1~~
35		1 ~~2~~	+
8		~~1~~	+
4		+	+
	23	1	1
	1	1 2	1 2
26		1 ~~2~~	
6		~~1~~	+
35		+	+
11		+	+
31		+	+

Results:

Line 1. + 19. Line clear.

Line 2. + 16. Line clear.

Running total: No write-off: + 71.

Write-off: + 60.

Backing BLACK. Both lines clear.

(N) B	(R) R	No write-off	Write-off
	7	1	1
	25	1 2	1 2
	5	1 2 3	1 2 3
	30	1 2 3 4	1 2 3 4
26		1 2 3 ~~4~~	1 2 3 ~~4~~
17		1 2 ~~3~~	1 2 ~~3~~
4		1 ~~2~~	
	9	1 2	1
	5	1 2 3	1 2
4		1 2 ~~3~~	
	9	1 2 3	1
	3	1 2 3 4	1 2
	1	1 2 3 4 5	1 2 3
	21	1 2 3 4 5 6	1 2 3 4

[Continued Overleaf

Continued from previous page]

Backing BLACK. Both lines clear.

(N) B	(R) R	No write-off							Write-off				
15		1	2	3	4	5	6̸		1	2	3	4̸	
31		1	2	3	4	5̸			1	2	3̸		
	14	1	2	3	4	5			1	2	3		
	14	1	2	3	4	5	6		1	2	3	4	
	27	1	2	3	4	5	6	7	1	2	3	4	5
17		1	2	3	4	5	6	7̸	1	2	3	4	5̸
	12	1	2	3	4	5	6	7	1	2	3	4	5
33		1	2	3	4	5	6	7̸	1	2	3	4	5̸
4		1	2	3	4	5	6̸		1	2	3	4̸	
7		1	2	3	4	5̸			1	2	3̸		
10		1	2	3	4̸								
6		1	2	3̸					+				
	19	1	2	3					1				
33		1	2	3̸					1̸				
	9	1	2	3					1				
	3	1	2	3	4				1	2			
28		1	2	3	4̸								

Results:
Line 1. + 14. Line outstanding 1 2 3.
Line 2. + 10. Line clear.

Running totals:
Line 1. + 85 units. Line outstanding 1 2 3.
Line 2. + 71 units. Line clear.

Backing BLACK. Line 1: 1 2 3. Line 2 clear

(N) B	(R) R	No write-off							Write-off	
22		1	2	3̸					+	
	36	1	2	3					1	
	5	1	2	3	4				1	2
35		1	2	3	4̸				—	
	19	1	2	3	4				1	
	1	1	2	3	4	5			1	2
13		1	2	3	4	5̸			—	
	12	1	2	3	4	5			1	
	18	1	2	3	4	5	6		1	2
2		1	2	3	4	5	6̸		—	
	34	1	2	3	4	5	6		1	
	9	1	2	3	4	5	6	7	1	2
29		1	2	3	5	5	6	7̸	—	

Backing BLACK. Line 1: 1 2 3. Line 2: 1 2.

(N) B	(R) R	No write-off	Write-off
	25	1 2 3 4 5 6 7	1
	16	1 2 3 4 5 6 7 8	1 2
	7	1 2 3 4 5 6 7 8 9	1 2 3
33		1 2 3 4 5 6 7 8 ~~9~~	1 2 ~~3~~
11		1 2 3 4 5 6 7 ~~8~~	—
	16	1 2 3 4 5 6 7 8	1
	18	1 2 3 4 5 6 7 8 9	1 2
	27	1 2 3 4 5 6 7 8 9 10	1 2 3
	21	1 2 3 4 5 6 7 8 9 10 11	1 2 3 4
	32	1 2 3 4 5 6 7 8 9 10 11 12	1 2 3 4 5
	1	1 2 3 4 5 6 7 8 9 10 11 12 13	1 2 3 4 5 6
8		1 2 3 4 5 6 7 8 9 10 11 12 ~~13~~	1 2 3 4 5 ~~6~~
28		1 2 3 4 5 6 7 8 9 10 11 ~~12~~	1 2 3 4 ~~5~~
	19	1 2 3 4 5 6 7 8 9 10 11 12	1 2 3 4 5
	36	1 2 3 4 5 6 7 8 9 10 11 12 13	1 2 3 4 5 6
	12	1 2 3 4 5 6 7 8 9 10 11 12 13 14	1 2 3 4 5 6 7
	23	1 2 3 4 5 6 7 8 9 10 11 12 13 14 15	1 2 3 4 5 6 7 8
	3	1 2 3 4 5 6 7 8 9 10 11 12 13 14 15 16	1 2 3 4 5 6 7 8 9

Result:
Line 1. + 9 units. Line runs from 1 to 16. (136 units.)
Line 2. + 4 units. Line runs from 1 to 9. (45 units.)

Running total:
Line 1. + 94 units with 136 outstanding = losing 42 units.
Line 2. + 75 units with 45 outstanding = winning 30 units.

The write-off principle scores notably here. It is true that the all-out method could have stopped earlier and shown a profit over and above that shown by write-off, but this final column which causes all the damage might have come earlier. Both players are to an extent fortunate in that, electing to back Black, they chose the right target. The genuine success for the write-off principle is better appreciated by noting that had this final column been the first, the difference between the two losses would have been greater. Write-off would have been losing 42 units. All-out would have been losing 127, treble the amount.

The experienced player, using write-off, would almost certainly have done far better than this.

For purposes of illustration the final column had to be played right through by both players, but the experienced player, having his apprehensions confirmed by that deviation at the beginning of the final column where he writes off two losses with one win no less than five times, would undoubtedly have said 'enough', taken his profit of 69 units at the third or fourth write-off, and looked around for a fresh target. The deviation was too clearly swinging away from Black to Red for a continuation to be attractive.

The all-out player might be experienced also but his decision was more difficult. Did he consider a change of target at the level of fourth write-off, his line is showing a total of 15–21 units. If he decides to scrap that amount now he would have done better to use write-off throughout.

The Paroli

This method tries to get good odds for a particular bet. A stake of 1 unit on an even chance position stands to win 1 unit, i.e. even money. Should the resultant 2 units which appear on the table when the bet is paid be permitted to remain, and again win, the result is 4 units, giving—superficially—odds of 3–1 instead of even money.

Should this be again left and again win the total would be 8 units, odds of 7–1 against a total liability of 1 unit.

With the latter position we are not immediately concerned, but it should be clear that odds of 3–1 against an even chance are not in reality obtainable. Having won the first coup, to let it ride is the exact equivalent of removing it and then staking a fresh bet of 2 units at even money. This of course, as will the bet let ride, be lost half the time. Nevertheless there are situations where this type of play becomes useful.

The Paroli of Two

Technically this does not exist. The Paroli gambit is, having won a coup, not merely to let the total ride but to increase it.

Stake 1 unit. It wins. On the table are 2 units. Add 1. Stake is now 3 units. It wins. 6 units are lifted. The profit is 4 units.

This is deceptive. The added unit makes no more profit than does a single unit for a single bet. 3 units out of the 4 units profit are directly due to the initial stake of 1 unit. This method of increasing the stake is therefore inefficient unless the added stake rides for at least two spins. A genuine Paroli must therefore be a minimum of three wins in succession.

The Paroli of Three

Stake 1 unit. It wins. Add 1 unit. Stake is 3 units. It wins. Table shows 6 units. Let it ride. It wins. Remove 12 units; profit 10 units.

Variation (non-technical)

Having won the second spin, 6 units show. Remove the stake, ensuring no loss. 4 units remain and may be considered to be House money, not personal capital at all. If this loses no apparent harm has been done; if it wins the profit is 8 units, for again—apparently— nothing. This variation however incorporates the same loss of efficiency as does the 'Paroli' of Two.

The Paroli of Four

Stake 1 unit. It wins. Add 1 unit.
Second coup wins. Table shows 6 units. Let it ride.
Third coup wins. Table shows 12 units. Remove 2 units, the total stake. If the fourth coup wins, the nett profit is 20 units.
This Paroli of four is a genuine gamble, but is nevertheless thoroughly sound in construction. The time to employ it is when runs of four are becoming common. To attempt this type of gambit when quick alternations of result are prevalent is obviously unwise.

Capital

Reasonable capital is required lest a run of non-success is encountered, but this 'reasonable' indicates number of units, not necessarily amount of money.

Recommended

The Paroli of Three

Drill

1. Wait until the wheel produces a run of five or more for any even chance position.
2. Subsequently back the dominant. Thus, should Red win five times in succession, wait until the table changes to show a win for Black and then back Black to produce a run of four. (One win has of course already gone, so the bet is for the next three spins.)

3. Having won, add a second stake, equivalent to the first.
4. Having won, let it ride.
5. Having won for the third time, lift the total, which will be twelve units and a profit of ten units.
6. If the bet loses, back the next dominant (here Red) again looking for that position to produce a run of four. If it fails return to Black, and so on.

Limit of Outlay

It may be thought advisable to set a limit to this play. Should the table swing back to a series of quick alternatives it should probably be abandoned after some half-dozen attempts. Otherwise, as the profit from success is 10 units, the play may not unreasonably be continued to that limit.

(N)	(R)	
B	R	
6		
11		
15		
20		
33		
	9	Black has won five times; Back Red.
17		1 unit lost. Back Black. (−1)
2		Black wins; add 1 unit.
	18	Black loses. Back Red. (−3)
24		Black wins; back Black. (−4)
4		Add 1 unit.
29		Black wins for the third time. Let it ride.
35		Black wins for the fourth time. (+6)

12 units are lifted; 6 units have been placed; profit is 6 units.
The cautious player might perhaps have lifted after three wins, thus clearing his loss line of 4 units and his included stake of 2 units, finishing all square.

Simple Reduction of Method

From time to time at the table it appears that the wheel persists in producing no singleton such as Nos. 9 and 18 above. This is the time to 'let it run' for one spin. When a bet is won, leave it. The situation is favourable and odds are 3–1 to the capital, a loss of only 1 unit to be accepted if this even money chance fails.

Increase of Initial Stake

If capital is available the initial stake on a Paroli may be increased with excellent prospects.

Spin 1. stake 3 units (or at discretion).

Spin 2. add 3 units more, a total outlay of 6 units.

Spin 3. let it ride. Should it win, 36 units are lifted.

If a decision is made to shoot for a Paroli of four the stake, 6 units, is best retrieved after Spin 3 has won, thus safeguarding the basic capital, and remaining with an expectation, should Spin 4 win, of 60 units profit.

The cautious player may play about with units in this situation, perhaps lifting 12 units when Spin No. 3 wins. This leaves 24 units of House money to play for a possible total profit of 54 units. (48 from Spin No. 4, 6 from Spin No. 3). Should Spin No. 4 lose, a reserve of 6 units has been gained.

Example of 'leaving it once'

(N)	(R)
B	R
4	
29	
31	
	18
	36
35	
2	
	3

At this stage the table appears to be producing double dominants at worst. Red may therefore be backed and, should it win, be permitted to remain to show a profit of 3 units if it wins again. If it loses, the loss is theoretically only 1 unit, and the procedure may be repeated with a higher stake if so desired. Other ways are available if it is considered that this loss should be recovered before a further positive play is made.

Playing for doubletons. (An analysis of a popular misconception.)

Another example of 'letting it ride', this time as a basic system, not merely an interpolated bet induced by circumstances.

Drill

Select a position and back it to produce a double winner. Stake 1 unit each spin, but when the selected position wins let it ride for a further spin.

Progression for Doubleton

Bet no.	Stake	Win if won	Lost if lost
1	1	3	1
2	1	2	2
3	1	1	3
4	2	3	5
5	2	1	7
6	3	2	10
7	4	2	14
8	5	1	19
9	7	2	26
10	9	1	35

Economy

Because a number of stakes are inevitably lost even while waiting for the first winner on the selected position, a complete Martingale progression is likely to prove too drastic, so a Split Martingale type, using a secondary line should be employed.

11	2	6	37
12	3	7	40
13	4	7	44
14	5	6	49
15	7	7	56
16	9	6	65
17	12	6	77

This line may be used until the first line has been cleared. When that happens reversion is made to the first line.

More economy

If these two lines are too heavy, a modified series may be used with a
primary line 1 1 1 2 2 3 4 and a secondary line 2 3 4 5 6. Backing
BLACK.

(N)	(R)	Stake	Line
B	R	1	
	27	1	1
33		let it ride	
24		wins	— Stake 1
	18	1	1
	18	1	1 1
26		let it ride	
	25	2	1 1 1
17		let it ride	
33		wins	— Stake 1
	16	1	1
22		let it ride	
	3	1	1 1
20		let it ride	
	5	2	1 1 1
6		let it ride	
	9	2	1 1 1 2
20		let it ride	
	0	imprisoned	
	5	3	1 1 1 2 2
4		let it ride	
10		wins	Stake 1
	36	1	1
31		let it ride	
8		wins	Stake 1
29		let it ride	
6		wins	Stake 1
	32	1	1
31		let it ride	
8		wins	Stake 1
29		let it ride	
6		wins	Stake 1
	32	1	1
4		let it ride	
	16	1	1 1
	1	2	1 1 1
26		let it ride	
35		wins	Stake 1
28		let it ride	
20		wins	Stake 1

(N)	(R)	Stake	Line
B	R		
8		let it ride	
	19	1	1
	23	1	1 1
10		let it ride	
	21	2	1 1 1
24			

This was a well chosen target showing a profit of 23 units, although a line is yet in being 1 1 1 the result of which cannot be known.

We use the same column but this time back what seems to be un-attractive in hindsight—RED.

This wins a unit swiftly but then produces something akin to disaster, a line 1 1 1 2 2 3 4 2 3 4 5 6 and, should we extend, endeavouring to recoup with more extravagant lines such as 3 4 5 6 7 8 followed by 4 6 8 10 those lines are also written before any allevia-tion arrives.

As with the Contra-Alembert therefore, this type of system ought to be played on both sides, not merely on one, because the choice of the right target is all-important, and to choose the wrong one is far more costly than to choose the right one is profitable.

Yet, referring to the section on The Immutable Law, we find that this is precisely the system erroneously advocated there.

The answer is clear—this method of letting the bet ride for a double win is excellent when used as an interpolated bet in circumstances which appear favourable. As a standard system it is not to be recom-mended, and analysis should deter devotees who have received advice somewhat less than sound.

The trouble so often has been that much of the writing on gaming has concentrated upon the esoteric to the disregard of simple logic, the result often being quite baffling to the average reader. Relevant to this practice of letting the bet run, we find; 'The bank's edge against a cover of 18 numbers is 5·26%.' (We don't know how this was calculated and perhaps prefer to remain in ignorance.) The con-tinuation is: 'Two players have one unit to lose. One places it three times and wins 3 units; the second places it once and lets it ride for three spins, thus winning 7 units. The sequence is exploited to the full. The first player is clearly not only inhibited by his fear of the 'law of large numbers' but has a different reaction to Cardano's law.'

Firstly, a three-timer can hardly be said to 'exploit a sequence to the full'. The only way to do that is to leave a stake until the win exceeds the House maximum, to withdraw the surplus and to let the equivalent of the maximum ride until a loss is incurred.

Secondly, simple arithmetic tells us that if these players remain consistent in their play and experience an exact average of results, their final scores will be equal. The man who stakes in single units will—bar the Zero effect—win exactly half his bets and so finish all square. The man who lets it ride for three spins will win 7 units precisely once in each eight plays, and also finish level.

The true difference between these men is that the first risks 1 unit on the first spin, 1 unit more on the second but knowing that even should he lose he has broken even, and 1 unit on the third, knowing that even should he lose he remains with a 1 unit profit. The second man stakes 1 unit on the first spin, 2 units on the second and 4 units on the third, all of it his own money, each time knowing that, should he lose, his capital is exhausted.

Thirdly, the average reader has little knowledge of the law of large numbers, may never have heard of Signor Cardano and, should he be advised to consult the magnum opus of M. Laplace on the laws of probability would almost certainly—just as did M. Laplace—come out of the same door as in he went, while, should he carry a detailed compendium of all these abstruse matters in his head as part of his everyday equipment, it would do him not a ha'porth of good when he sat down at a Roulette table.

Which is why we concentrate on the practical, presenting theory only when it is necessary to demolish it.

The Doubleton Progression by sections

This method is far more controlled than was the previous one, and will have more appeal to the thinking player.

Drill

Select an even chance position which tends to produce doubletons. Stake 1 unit three times. When a stake wins, let it ride for a further spin.

Write a line consisting of the overall result. Thus, should a win be made against two losses, the line is merely plus 1 unit and need not be written, but if three losses are incurred the line is 1 1 1. Select another position which appears attractive, and do similarly except with a stake of 2 units.

If the eventual line extends menacingly, as perhaps 1 1 1 2 2 2 3 3 3 4 4 4 start a fresh line using two plays only at the same stake but four plays per section, commencing with 1 unit again.

The progression is: 1122, 3344, 5566. All wins in such progressions are put towards the cancelling of the previous line. Nothing is considered to be, or put aside as profit until this has been done.

Switching the Win

(N)	(R)	
B	R	
13		
	18	
24		
	9	At this stage, the intermittence seems to have taken charge, and a stake on its continuance is reasonable. Back Black. Should it win, switch the resultant 2 units to Red. Financial conditions are identical with the procedure which 'lets it ride'.

Recovery of loss on Paroli

1 unit is staked and wins. 1 unit is added but the bet loses, showing a loss of 2 units. If we decide to recover this before attempting another Paroli it may be done by using 2 units as the start of a progression; 2 3 6 12 24 etc. using perhaps five hypothetical bets, or to recover the units one by one in complete progressions 1 2 4 8 etc. A Martingale line (Split) may also be used, and we shall see this shortly.

Drill for Zero during a Paroli

Stake 1 unit. If Zero wins it is imprisoned. If it be liberated, decide whether to remove it or leave it. The point to consider is that now the position will have to win once extra for the Paroli to succeed.

If Zero wins after a single win for the position, 1 unit has already been added, so 3 units are imprisoned. The best action is to leave it. If it is liberated, lift the 3 units, taking 1 unit of profit, awaiting a fresh opportunity for the play.

If Zero wins after the position has won twice, 6 units are imprisoned. Share them, taking 1 unit profit.

The 'Immutable' Law

Having seen the method of 'Leaving it once' this may be a suitable point at which to demolish a theory which has taken remarkable hold. For a century thousands of players have succumbed to the attraction of what has been variously called the 'Immutable' the 'Inescapable' the 'Inevitable' etc., a 'law' purporting to be a natural, arithmetical derivation from the Law of Averages.

This 'law' has been published in good faith many times and has probably cost a lot of people a lot of money. We quote:

'Of a million spins, disregarding the Zero, each colour will win approximately half. After each win it has precisely an even chance to win again. Therefore runs of two consecutive winners will—on perfect average—be precisely half as many as single wins. In natural continuation, runs of three will be precisely half as many as runs of two, runs of four half as many as runs of three and so on.'

'The expectation of runs from each colour in one million spins is therefore:

Runs of 2	250,000
3	125,000
4	62,500
5	31,250
6	15,625

and so on down to an expectation of 19 runs of 19.'

This 'law', so presented, carries an air of authority, of arithmetical exactitude and of serious hope for system construction. Here is an example of the type of system which has been based upon it.

Preamble: We intend to place 100 initial bets. Because our 'law' has made no allowance for Zero however, we will allot to Zero no less than four wins during that 100 bet series for reasons of safety. This leaves 96 bets to be won by Black and Red between them. On average 48 will be won by each. According to our 'law' each colour therefore, having won 48 times, will win twice in succession 24 times. This being satisfactory for our purposes we take it no further.

Principle: We intend to back both colours simultaneously. We intend to replace each losing bet but to leave each winning bet to ride for one further spin.

Outlay: At Spin 1 we stake 1 unit on each colour, a total of 2 units outlay. For each of the next 99 spins we simply replace the single unit which has been lost, a total of 99 units outlay, 101 in all. When Spin No. 100 is decided, we end our series, not replacing the losing bet but lifting 2 units from the winning colour. The total possible outlay on the series is therefore 99 units.

Profit: Black will win twice in succession 24 times. So will Red. Thus a double win will arrive 48 times, and on the table will appear a total of 4 units. Of this we lift 3.

Conclusion: We lift 48 × 3 = 144 units

We place   99

             45 units automatic profit.

Rebuttal of Objection

That a perfect average may not obtain for the colours is immaterial. They may produce their ration of 24 double wins or the écart may perhaps cause Red to win 36, Black only 12. This is extreme but makes no difference. The same 48 double wins are there and the same 45 units of profit is made.

Genuine analysis

This 'law' presents an optical illusion and the system derived from it is not only fallacious but badly constructed. Why for example should we replace the losing bet at every spin, taking 100% risk of Zero winning? The same arithmetical result is obtained by placing 2 units on the winning colour—providing the right number of double wins is produced.

Any set number of spins comprises a set number of columns. A million spins is roughly 27,000 columns. If a million spins produce

500,000 double wins, each column must produce eighteen double wins and that average must be permanent and consistent. Let a colour fail to do this in one single column and some subsequent column must provide an extra doubleton in order to maintain the average. As this means at least 38 spins while the column contains only 37 (36 while we are disregarding the Zero) the thing is fundamentally impossible.

Justification for this 'law' could only arrive were every column to consist of nothing but doubletons or runs of multiples of two, i.e. of even length, as, for example:

$$\begin{array}{ll} 10 & \\ 28 & \\ & 5 \\ & 19 \\ 13 & \\ 15 & \\ 33 & \\ 11 & \\ & 9 \\ & 36 \end{array}$$

A single run of uneven length would automatically make eighteen doubletons impossible.

$$\begin{array}{ll} 11 & \\ 6 & \\ & 5 \\ 22 & \end{array}$$

Once that No. 5 is in isolation, there remain only 35 spins from our 36 to produce eighteen doubletons. It is not enough.

Even the spin we allot to Zero will ruin the theory:

$$\begin{array}{lll} 28 & & \\ & 19 & \\ 0 & & \\ & & 5 \\ 6 & & \end{array}$$

This 19–5 was going to be a double win for Red, but the interposition of the Zero has not only given the Zero its allotted spin in the column but has prevented one genuine doubleton from materialising. Considering this small point alone three spins have been used up, leaving only 34 in the column to produce eighteen doubletons, again impossible.

Runs of uneven length also ruin the theory:

4

6

19

1

36

31

Once three spins are in that column as a run, isolated by wins for Black, we have one doubleton but one spin scheduled to be part of another doubleton is no longer available. Once again the arithmetic of the 'law' is ruined.

So, when this 'law' states that of a million spins won by colours, disregarding the Zero (and the Zero effect of disruption), there will be half-a-million doubletons, it is totally wrong. The number of doubletons in a million such spins can only be calculated after we have deducted not merely the Zero allotment, but the number of doubletons invalidated by the interpolation of the Zero, the number of coups which come at the end of runs of uneven length and the number of coups which result in single wins being isolated. (And there are frequently a dozen or more of these in a column.) By the time we have taken all these into account our original million spins have been sadly reduced.

It is true, however, that of the initial spins won by a colour, that colour will produce half that number of doubletons (disregarding the Zero and also its disruptive effect), (see Table of Frequencies), but to set a number in advance is to ruin the logic of the argument and to produce a correct-seeming conclusion from a false premise. Thus, instead of a 100-bet series producing 48 double wins it is far more likely to produce something like 30, and the proposed system must over a period inevitably lose.

Were the 'law' to be accurate we could construct a far better system anyway. All that is needed is to wait until a colour wins and then back it for the maximum. As it would have to produce a doubleton the win is automatic.

It is untrue that figures can be produced to prove anything. What is true is that figures can be produced to prove anything to the satisfaction of those who do not bother to analyse them for a possible fallacy. People not scientists may be 'blinded by science' because they cannot analyse the proposition. But there is no reason for people to be blinded by simple arithmetic, and the sad thing about this 'law' is that it has deceived so many people for so long, and must have caused enormous losses.

The Sleeper: Single Numbers

The Sleeper is the twin of the hypothetical bet but is used for positions which carry greater odds. Faith is placed rather in the Table of Frequencies than in the Law of Averages—wisely. The method for single numbers requires a good capital and enormous patience. It is however intrinsically profitable, while the other sleeping targets offer more frequent chances.

Each single number should on average win once in each 37 spins. If a number has failed to win for 74 spins it is therefore not unlikely that it will appear in the next 74. The odds against its doing so remain the same 35–1 although it is doubtful if a bookmaker could be induced to offer them. Such a 'horse' would probably be installed as a second favourite at least, and the odds against it seriously reduced. It is attractive, therefore, to be able to make a bet which a bookmaker would be unlikely to accept.

Every Roulette table issues cards to players who desire to keep a record. Sometimes these are of full length—37 spaces—sometimes of less. If a player wishes to keep a record of sleepers it is therefore advisable either to patronise a casino which gives full length cards or to prepare his own.

Cards are easily constructed from squared paper available at any office stationer. The card should be numbered from 0–36. As each number wins it is ticked. At the end of each column it will then become obvious which numbers have failed to appear.

One advantage in backing single numbers is that the stake need not increase by leaps and bounds as it does with progressions on even chances. At odds of 35–1 a single unit may be placed 35 times in succession and still show a profit if it wins on the last of these.

This, however, seems to be a lot of work for very little. The win, mathematically, is likely to come earlier, between Spins No. 23 and 24 on average expectation, so the average profit should be some 11 or 12 units, but we will nevertheless give a progression of only 30 1-unit bets, so that the smallest win is not quite contemptible.

Bets Nos. 1–30: stake 1 unit.

If Bet No. 1 wins, the profit is 35 units, and this diminishes by 1 unit on each successive bet. Thus a win at Bet No. 16 will give 35–15 = 20 units profit.

Bets 31–45: stake 2 units.
Maximum profit Bet No. 31 = 40 units.
Minimum profit Bet No. 45 = 12 units.
Bets 46–56: stake 3 units.
Maximum profit Bet 46: 45 units.
Minimum profit Bet 56: 15 units.
Bets 57–64: stake 4 units.
Maximum profit Bet 57: 47 units.
Minimum profit Bet 64: 19 units.
Bets 65–72: stake 5 units.
Maximum profit Bet 65: 50 units.
Minimum profit Bet 72: 15 units.
Capital required for progression of 72 bets: 165 units.

Adjusting stake to House maximum

Should a 72-bet progression be used and extra capital be available, the size of initial unit may be adjusted to the House maximum. If an *en plein* bet of five pounds is permitted, a basic unit of one pound may be employed. If the en plein maximum is only two pounds, the basic unit may not be more than one-fifth of this.

Increasing the length of the Progression

Bets 73–78: stake 6 units.
Maximum profit Bet 73: 50 units.
Minimum profit Bet 78: 20 units.
Bets 78–82: stake 7 units.
Maximum profit Bet 78: 49 units.
Minimum profit Bet 82: 23 units.
Bets 83–86: stake 8 units.
Maximum profit Bet 83: 49 units.
Minimum profit Bet 86: 25 units.
Bets 87–90: stake 9 units.

Maximum profit Bet 87: 52 units.
Minimum profit Bet 90: 25 units.
Bets 91–94: stake 10 units.
Maximum profit Bet 91: 55 units.
Minimum profit Bet 94: 11 units.
With a stake of 10 units the basic unit must, of course, not be higher than one-tenth of the permitted House en plein maximum.

The progression continues

Bets 95–97: stake 11 units.
Maximum profit Bet 95: 46 units.
Minimum profit Bet 97: 24 units.
Bets 98–100: stake 12 units.
Maximum profit Bet 98: 48 units.
Minimum profit Bet 100: 24 units.

Construction of a progression

The final bet at any specific stake must be capable of showing a result satisfactory to the player. This may be a win of a single unit. It may even be in the nature of an insurance bet, making no profit. (An example of this would be to place 36 bets at a stake of 1 unit initially. If the win comes at Bet 36, the stake is lifted and the profit, 35 units, exactly cancels the previous 35 losses.) This again seems to be a lot of work for little, yet the odds are long—precisely 35–1—against that one particular bet being the winning one, while its presence in the progression gives us an extra bet and therefore a better chance not to lose our capital.

This would perhaps be the tactic of the player who desires to protect his capital come what may. He may even add an extra bet at the same stake to show a loss of 1 unit, again lengthening his progression and banking that the win will not occur at that precise point. Once over that little hump his next stake of 2 units will restore his profit, although the interpolation will naturally reduce the eventual win by 1 unit.

The progression may thus be extended without increasing the capital outlay; simply interpolating bets where space exists, or even, as we have just seen, where space does not exist. Five extra bets to show a profit may be inserted into the given progression at the 1 unit stake. There is room elsewhere for interpolation. There is also room at the end for extension. The progression may continue indefinitely with its only limits the available capital and the ratio of the House minimum stake to the House maximum.

The Long Sleep

It is rare for a number to fail to appear in as many as five columns—185 spins. Nevertheless warning must be given that no capital is 100% secure. Records are always being broken, while the more the game is played the more opportunities present themselves for this very thing.

If disaster does arrive in an extended progression of this kind it will certainly be bad luck, but it must be appreciated that bad luck is part of the game, and that it may arrive for anyone. (The longest 'sleep' we have seen is 242 spins.)

To cope with 242 spins we need a three-column sleeper (111 spins) plus a progression of 131 spins. Playing with this progression we see that it needs extension by 31 bets. The best way to do this is to wait for a four-column sleeper which automatically gives 248 spins. This costs nothing. If less waiting time is desired, resort must be made to a balance between interpolation and increase of capital. This may again be aided by waiting a little longer, not necessarily another full column. We may quite validly wait for three columns and an extra dozen or so spins.

All these points must be considered by the serious player before he attempts to beat the table. He must also be thoroughly familiar with his manual drill. A player selecting a progression and rushing straight to the table to use it will almost certainly make some foolish mistake of drill which may prove expensive.

A card should be prepared, showing the actual bets to be made. Each one should be crossed off immediately it has been placed. To do this at a precise moment is important. Routine is essential; a strict adherence to that routine equally so. This is of course *work*, but that is what we promised. It is the task of the would-be winner to work. The losers are the people who go to casinos to *play*.

Here is the progression laid out readily for individual crossing off.

1 1 1 1 1 1 1 1 1 1 1 1 1 1 1 1 1 1 1 1 1 1 1 1 1 1 1 1 1 1 1 1
2 2 2 2 2 2 2 2 2 2 2 2 2 2 2 2 3 3 3 3 3 3 3 3 3 3 3 4 4 4 4
4 4 4 4 5 5 5 5 5 5 5 6 6 6 6 6 6 7 7 7 7 7 8 8 8 8 9 9 9 9
10 10 10 10 11 11 11 12 12 12 ~~17~~

The first nine bets have been placed and duly crossed off. The number being backed has been inserted at the side.

This record sheet—a job for the office typewriter—should carry half-a-dozen or so of these pro-formae, depending upon the length of session the player expects to play.

Time-limit

While waiting for a single number target to appear some other play may be embarked upon. What is important however is that once the progression has started it does not get shot down in the middle. Nothing can be more infuriating than to reach, say, Bet No. 84 or so and to hear the inspector announce: 'Last three spins.'

Therefore the player should make sure that his table will remain in play for the time necessary for him to complete his progression. 'Get there early' seems to be a good motto.

Multiple targets

Several numbers may be backed simultaneously with the progression. It is important however to appreciate that a larger capital may be necessary. The crossing off will be simple with targets which present themselves at the same time, and one pro-forma will do for them combined, but targets coming in while we are in the middle of a progression on a previous one will need care. *The Zero* does not affect the progression in any way. It is simply a lost bet as is any other wrong number, so the next stake is placed in the normal way.

This record card gives four double columns for Black and Red. Three only are used. The first, together with the left-hand margin, is used to denote which numbers have won in the respective columns, the margin taking the first, Black the second, Red the third column. As each number wins it is ticked in the appropriate column. Glancing

Imperial Casino

Date: ....

✓	#	B	R	B	R	B	R	B	R
	0		✓	17		6			18
✓	1		✓	22		20		26	
✓	2		✓	4			7	6	
✓	3	✓	✓	26		6			23
✓	4	✓		17			3	26	
	5	✓	✓		14	17			12
	6	✓	✓	4		33		31	
	7	✓	✓	22			23		12
	8	✓		29		29			7
	9	✓	✓	31			30		25
	10		✓		1	26			16
	11	✓	✓		3	15			3
	12		✓	28			32		27
	13		✓	17			5		16
✓	14				19		18		32
✓	15	✓	✓		34	33		6	
✓	16	✓	✓	15		31		13	
✓	17	✓		17			30	15	
✓	18	✓	✓	28			8		9
✓	19				1		36	31	
	20	✓			19		9	2	
	21	✓			23		30		18
✓	22	✓	✓	24		11			7
✓	23	✓	✓		36	28		29	
✓	24				30	15		10	
	25		✓		19		6	0	
✓	26	✓		15		4			32
✓	27	✓	✓		32	22		4	
✓	28	✓	✓		23		21		34
✓	29	✓	✓	17		29			1
✓	30	✓		4			27	33	
✓	31	✓	✓	24		31		28	
✓	32	✓	✓		14		36		3
	33	✓	✓		16	33			32
✓	34	✓	✓		27		16	22	
	35			2			3		5
✓	36	✓		22			34	11	

at the first line of ticks we see a large gap; not one single number from 5–13 has appeared. This immediately gives us possible targets, not for single numbers but for the sixain 4, 5, 6, 7, 8, 9; the sixain 7, 8, 9, 10, 11, 12; the transversals 7, 8, 9; 10, 11, 12; 4, 5, 6; the chevaux 4–5, 4–7, 5–6, 5–8, 6–9, 7–10. 7–8, 8–9. 8–11, 9–12, 10–11. There is also a sleeping cheval at 20–21. Isolated numbers sleeping for the one column are 25, 33 and 35. And Zero.

We will have progressions for all these positions later. For the moment we seek single numbers. When the second column is concluded sleeping single numbers are 0, 10, 12, 13, 25 and 35. At the end of the third column however only one remains, No. 35. If the end of that column is our moment for commencing a progression, this is the target.

In passing, we note that Nos. 14, 19 and 24 have now been sleeping for the second and third columns, so may provide another target shortly. The transversal 19, 20, 21 is also sleeping, as are the chevaux 19–20, 17–20 and 14–17.

This accumulation of adjacent numbers might entice us to place a blanketing series of bets, as:

10	11	12
13	14 ●	15
16	17 ●	18
● 19	● 20	● 21
22	23	24

If No. 14 wins we win 17 units and lose 4 = +13.

17	34	3 = +31.
19	28	3 = +25.
20	62	1 = +61.
21	28	3 = +25.

No. 14 = one cheval
No. 17 = two chevaux
No. 19 = one cheval, one transversal
No. 20 = three chevaux, one transversal
No. 21 = one cheval, one transversal

This is not serious work, but it is quite reasonable Roulette, suitable for the player who has adequate capital at his disposal and is not averse to an occasional gamble.

Looking for lesser profit but more frequent wins, we could use carrés instead of chevaux, as:

Carrés, being four numbers against the two of a cheval, should win twice as often.

No. 13 wins:	Win 8	Lose 6 = +2
No. 14	76	5 = +11
No. 15	8	6 = +2
No. 16	16	5 = +11
No. 17	32	3 = +29
No. 18	16	5 = +11
No. 19	27	4 = +23
No. 20	43	2 = +41
No. 21	27	4 = +23

Single Numbers in Rotation

If we back a number completely at random the average expectation for it to appear is ·693 of the odds against it appearing immediately. This means that—on average—it will win about Spin No. 23 or 24. This suggests a leisurely method of attack which will often prove very successful.

Drill

Stake 1 unit on No. 1 and continue to do so for 24 spins or until it wins. A decision having been reached, do the same for No. 2 *unless it has already won.* If it has, select the next lowest number which has not yet won. Back this in similar fashion—1 unit stake for 24 spins. The play on every number will automatically provide extra sleeping time for the numbers which follow.

Practice Column Test

If we play this against the Practice Columns we find:

Number backed	Wins at	Lose	Profit. Running Total
1	Spin 4		32
2	3		65
3	16		85
6		24	61
8	11		86
14		24	62
20	2		96
32	19		113

Obviously a highly successful essay. We were, however, fortunate in getting home so soon with our early numbers. The whole sequence has taken 87 spins, probably an hour at an American table without cashier.

Single numbers in Rotation; guaranteed sleeping time; permutation of progressions

This method lends itself to separate book-keeping as does the Zero, calculating efficacy not session by session but over an extended period.

Drill

Write in the numbers from 0–36 as shown on p. 104. Here, however, it will not be necessary to use the first two colour-columns; the margin will be adequate by itself.
Play the first column in a suitable spin-to-spin way, ticking off the numbers as they appear. At the end of the column the numbers which

have not won will be obvious, and the lowest of them is chosen unless the wheel seems to be giving preference to high numbers; then it may be decided to change the order of selection.

Back the chosen number for 24 successive spins or until it has won. Having reached a decision make the next selection of number and back this for only 20 spins. The period occupied by the previous number will provide automatic sleeping time for this second number, plus, of course, the full column first played.

Having reached another decision, select the third number and back it for 16 spins only. If further numbers remain after the third decision, back these again for 16 spins only.

The standard stake throughout will be 1 unit.

Progression

If the series shows an overall loss, repeat the whole procedure using a stake of 2 units. If the second series shows a loss, repeat once more with a stake of 3 units.

Limit of progression

If the outstanding loss is less than 24 units after any series, use Series 1, i.e. a stake of 1 unit; if it is over 24 but less than 60 use Series 2, a stake of 2 units; if it is over 60 use a stake of 3 units.

Capital

A reasonable capital is required—basically 360 units—but may not be needed. The account should be carried forward from session to session. Losses will inevitably occur but overall results should be good. The system is therefore recommended to the regular player.

Ancillary

Providing the player is fully experienced and has his recording routine thoroughly taped, the entire system may be employed as an ancillary method, using a different method for the major part of play.

There is plenty of opportunity for this as the spin to spin drill merely consists of trailing along patiently with a flat stake on a selected number. This could—will—become boring if unrelieved by other methods, and while it is the duty of the serious player to be capable of sustaining such periods of boredom, there is no reason why he should do so if he can banish them by the use of different and concurrent plays.

The Sleeping Cheval

Two numbers in conjunction produce on average two wins per column of 37 spins. The equivalent of four hypothetical bets is therefore two complete columns. Extra safety may be obtained by waiting longer, and the experienced player will undoubtedly prefer to do this because, accustomed to the routine at the table, his own various drills having become automatic, he has plenty of other targets to occupy him.

This waiting time may be very comfortably extended almost indefinitely if there are two chevaux sleeping after two columns. The progression is then deferred until only one remains.

Bet No.	Stake	Loss of lost	Win if won
	PROGRESSION FOR SLEEPING CHEVAL		
1	1	1	17
2	1	2	16
3	1	3	15
4	1	4	14
5	1	5	13
6	1	6	12
7	1	7	11
8	1	8	10
9	1	9	9
10	1	10	8
11	1	11	7
12	1	12	6
13	1	13	5
14	1	14	4
15	1	15	3
16	1	16	2
17	2	18	18
18	2	20	16
19	2	22	14
20	2	24	12
21	2	26	10
22	2	28	8
23	2	30	6
24	2	32	4
25	3	35	19

Bet No.	Stake	Loss of lost	Win if won
		PROGRESSION FOR SLEEPING CHEVAL	
26	3	38	16
27	3	41	13
28	3	44	10
29	3	47	7
30	3	50	4
31	4	54	18
32	4	58	14
33	4	60	10
34	4	66	6
35	5	71	19
36	5	76	14
37	5	81	9
38	5	86	4
39	6	92	18
40	6	98	12
41	6	104	6
42	7	111	15
43	7	118	8
44	8	126	18
45	8	134	10
46	9	143	19
47	9	152	10
48	10	162	18
49	10	172	8

The progression may be extended at will provided the capital is available and the House maximum is not reached. The prepared record card for cheval progressions is:

```
1 1 1 1 1 1 1 1 1 1 1 1 1 1 1 1 1                     Five bets already
2 2 2 2 2 2 2 2 3 3 3 3 3 3 4 4   11-14              placed.
4 4 5 5 5 5 6 6 6 7 7 8 8 9 9 10 10
```

The card will of course have a number of these numeral pro-formae ready for use.

Alternative: Split Progression

Instead of a single progression which naturally depends upon one single result, whether one particular sleeping cheval behaves normally or produces a pathological coma, sleeping for what to the player will appear for ever, the progression may be made to depend

upon the result of a series of shortened progressions, as, for example:
Stake 1 unit for the first 16 bets. If the cheval still fails to win,
abandon it. Wait for a fresh target. When that arrives stake 2 units
for the first 16 bets. Failing again, abandon that and wait for another
target, against which a stake of 4 units for the 16 bets will be placed.
The eventual win may or may not show an overall profit, depending
naturally upon whether the progression won early or late. If it does,
the matter is closed. If it does not, the immediate profit is deducted
from the outstanding loss and a new target is attacked with a 16-bet
progression of 2 units, continuing in this manner until the slate has
been wiped clean.

The point at which to terminate the original progression if this
method is to be adopted is at the discretion of the individual player.
He may use a first line of 6 bets only if he prefers that, or may, at the
other extreme, stop at Bet No. 32 etc. This will depend basically upon
the available capital.

The Sleeping Transversal

This is always an attractive target, affording an opportunity for a reasonable progression after a number of spins fail to produce a win. We may treat it as we do even chances, using four hypothetical bets as analogous to a sleep of 48 spins.

Each transversal should—on average—win once in each twelve spins. (Precise average: 3 in 37.) If one fails to do this in 48 spins, it has slept for a similar time to an even chance which has failed to win in four successive spins. The length of slumber may be read quite easily from the card we used for single numbers etc. The transversal may then be backed with a progression and a reasonable expectation of winning shortly. Odds: 11–1.

Bet	Stake	Total capital	Amount won if this spin wins
1	1	1	11
2	1	2	10
3	1	3	9
4	1	4	8
5	1	5	7
6	1	6	6
7	1	7	5
8	1	8	4
9	1	9	3
10	1	10	2
11	1	11	1
12	2	13	11
13	2	15	9
14	2	17	7
15	2	19	5
16	2	21	3
17	3	24	12
18	3	27	9
19	3	30	6
20	3	33	3
21	4	37	11
22	4	41	7
23	4	45	3

Bet	Stake	Total capital	Amount won if this spin wins
24	5	50	10
25	5	55	5
26	6	61	11
27	6	67	5
28	7	74	10
29	7	81	3
30	8	89	7
31	9	98	10
32	10	108	12
33	10	118	2

Improvement of chance may be obtained simply by waiting for a longer sleep. This, precisely as with hypothetical bets, may be manipulated to reduce the capital, perhaps allowing two full columns for the sleep, and cutting the progression to 24 bets or, of course, any combination of these at discretion.

Transversals, however, rarely sleep for two full columns, which is a point to make this progression even more attractive.

The recording card to be prepared for this progression, so that no mistake is made in the actual staking is:

```
1 1 1 1 1 1 1 1 1 1 2 2 2 2 2
3 3 3 3 4 4 4 5 5          7–9
1 1 1 1 1 1 1 1 1 1 1 2 2 2 2 2
3 3 3 3 4 4 4 5 5
1 1 1 1 1 1 1 1 1 1 1 2 2 2 2 2
3 3 3 3 4 4 4 5 5
```

plus as many more pro-formae as the player desires or expects to use. The transversal backed may be written in at the side, as in the first example which has already placed thirteen bets.

When checking on the sleeping transversal it should be remembered that three consecutive numbers only constitute a transversal if the final one is a multiple of three. A series 5–6–7 although consecutive is not a transversal. Even though all three numbers are sleeping for the desired period they should not be backed as a transversal. They may be backed individually by placing a chip on each but this is an entirely different bet. It means that we are no longer backing a transversal but three single numbers, and the expectation of arrival for each is three times as long as it is for the numbers combined. The progression on each must be a progression aimed at a single number, not at a transversal, and, theoretically at least, all three might run to near the limit, thus demanding a triple, single number capital.

Series of graduated Progressions for Sleeping Transversal

This method demands some book-keeping but is eminently sound. Because of the time-factor the entire series may have to be carried forward through a number of sessions.

Drill

Having found a target, stake 1 unit for 11 bets.
Having lost these, follow with 2 units for 11 bets.
Having lost these also, follow with 3 units for 11 bets.
This gives a capital requirement of 66 units against the 118 units demanded by the complete progression previously shown. It uses the same number of bets but carries no guarantee of overall gain. The third series becomes an insurance series against the first and second, clearing the entire loss provided it wins with its first bet.
Should it win later, the first two series may be considered cleared, and the outstanding loss will be the stakes of 3 units lost in the present series. Thus, should Series 3 win at the fourth bet, three of its bets have been lost; the first and second series have been cleared but an outstanding line of 9 units remains uncleared.
This may in its turn be cleared by a further series, perhaps of 2 unit stakes, perhaps 3 unit stakes, this at the discretion of the player to accord with his capital availability.
Series such as this may be continued, increasing the stake each time up to the limit of available capital, this resulting in a 3 unit insurance series followed by (perhaps) a 4 unit under-insurance series and so on. Providing adequate capital is available this method must be recommended. Good book-keeping is important; patience is essential.

The Sleeping Sixain

Allowing one win for the Zero in each column of 37 spins, each Sixain should on average win six times per column. Translating this into the equivalent of hypothetical bets a progression on a sleeping sixain may be started after 24 spins.

The odds are only 5–1 so it will be a fairly short progression unless we permit the capital outlay to rise steeply.

Progression for Sixain

Bet No.	Stake	Loss if lost	Gain if won
1	1	1	5
2	1	2	4
3	1	3	3
4	1	4	2
5	1	5	1
6	2	7	5
7	2	9	3
8	2	11	1
9	3	14	4
10	3	17	1
11	4	21	3
12	5	26	4
13	6	32	4
14	7	39	3
15	8	47	1
16	10	57	3

It may be considered wise to permit the progression to lapse and be abandoned after Bet No. 13, accepting a loss of 32 units. This 13-bet progression completes one full column of 37 spins when the sleep of 24 spins is included. It is rare for a sixain to sleep for an entire column. It does happen, as does everything, so must be kept in mind. There are alternative methods for handling the situation.

Our example column certainly shows a sleeping Sixain but that is simply because it was selected in order to do so.

Recovery

Should it be decided to abandon after the loss of 32 units, this may be noted and an attempt made later to recover. The record card will show a further 24-bet sleeper at some time, and then the progression is repeated but this time with a stake of 2 units, thus actually commencing a progression within a progression. If this wins at, say, Bet No. 11, 6 units have been won instead of 3. The recorded loss is then reduced to 29 units, and the other 3 units placed in the normal day average. Such a loss may by this means be cleared entirely in time—a number of sessions naturally!

The bet record for the sixain is:

```
1 1 1 1 1 2 2 2     1 1 1 1 1 2 2 2      1 1 1 1 1 2 2 2
3 3 4 5 6 7 8 10     3 3 4 5 6 7 8 10      3 3 4 5 6 7 8 10
     7–12
```

The first record has already placed three bets on the sixain 7, 8, 9, 10, 11, 12.

Quicker Recovery

Having experienced a loss, as above, and desiring to clear it more decisively, the sleeping time may be extended, waiting for a full column or more before commencing the progression, which now may start with any figure considered suitable, an initial stake of 4 or 5 units perhaps.

Graduated Progressions

As with the Sleeping Transversal, graduated progressions may be undertaken, using a 1 unit stake for the first five bets, a 2 unit stake for the second five and so on, carrying the principle right through insurance and under-insurance series. With the sixain the stake will naturally rise far more quickly than with the transversal, the obverse of that medal being that the expectation of appearance is twice as soon. Book-keeping is therefore likely to be minimal, although it is sensible to allot a page in the ledger to the method.

Once again the 3 unit series clears the first and second series entirely, leaving outstanding only the lost bets in its own progression. A 4 units series will clear the first and third series, leaving outstanding the second series plus the bets lost within itself. We are here in genuine under-insurance play.

If this actual situation arrives the choice of subsequent stake will depend upon the amount remaining outstanding. The second series is 10 units lost; there are, say, three stakes of 4 units lost; a total of 22 units. To clear this it seems reasonable to drop down to the 3 unit stake if conservation of capital is important, to rest with a 4 unit stake if capital is readily available.

Sleeping finals

This is an attractive method for players who like to back numbers. It starts as an ancillary method but while in use must be allotted precedence over the basic system.

It consists of backing Finals which have not appeared for 28 spins. This number is chosen because it roughly equates four hypothetical bets. Each Final has a number of chances to appear in ten spins, ten the criterion because there are ten Finals—0–9; those below 7 having four chances, these 7 and above having three. But a particular number from 0–9 may be expected to appear once in a series of ten—if we are to lump these results together—and its actual expectation to appear is at the seventh spin. Four series of seven, giving 28 spins in which it has not appeared, may be said to equal four hypothetical bets.

The Final is backed for precisely nine spins, which completes a full column of 37 spins, and each column is taken in isolation.

The required capital is not small if a progression is used, and, as this is advisable, players should not adventure if a fair capital is not at hand. If it is, the method must be recommended.

Drill

Make a note of the final numbers as they appear. When there are nine spaces left in the column and one Final has not yet won, back it for the remaining spins in that column.

If it fails to win, back the next target with a progression. This may include insurance or under-insurance, just as may progressions in series with transversals and sixains. Nevertheless chances are so good that caution is vital only if the capital is in danger.

We will play right through our series of Practice Columns p. 212 using the method. We will use an insurance at first with an initial series of nine bets at 1 unit per number, a second series at 1 unit, (insurance) and a third series (under insurance unless it wins its first bet) of 2 units.

Notation

The numbers 0–9 are written down and crossed off as they appear.
If at Spin No. 28 one number has not yet been crossed off, it provides
a target.

Practice Columns

Column 1

The 28th spin gives us a win for No. 21 and as yet no Final 8 has
won. That therefore provides our target for the next nine spins.
Being over 6 it requires three chips per spin, our numbers being
8, 18 and 28.

No. 28 wins on the sixth spin, losing us 15 units on the first five and
2 units on the sixth; winning 35 units on the sixth; showing a profit
of 18 units.

Column 2

This provides no target. We therefore carry on with our staple
system and wait for the next column.

Column 3

The 28th spin gives us a win for No. 11 and as yet no Final 3 has
won. That therefore provides our target for the next nine spins.
Being under 7 it requires 4 chips per spin, our numbers being 3, 13,
23, 33.

No. 23 wins on the seventh spin, losing us 24 units on the first six,
3 units on the seventh; winning 35 units on the seventh; showing a
profit of 8 units.

Column 4

The 28th spin is won by No. 31. Final 0 has not yet appeared, so
provides our target, 4 chips per spin, and wins immediately, losing
3 units, winning 35 units to show a profit of 32 units.

Column 5

This provides no target, so our staple system regains its priority.

Column 6

Again no target.

Column 7

No. 7 wins at Spin No. 28, leaving us with a target of Final 3, 4 chips per spin, winning at Spin No. 4, losing 12 units on the first three, 3 units on the fourth, winning 35 units on the fourth, showing a profit of 20 units.

Column 8

No. 34 wins at Spin No. 28, giving us a target of Final 0, 4 chips per spin. This loses, showing a loss of 36 units.

Note: We do not continue to back Final 0, but wait for the next target in order to attack it with the second of our lines.

Column 9

No. 15 wins at Spin No. 28 giving us two targets, Final 7 and Final 0. This Final 0 was our previous losing target. Perhaps it intends to sleep like Rip van Winkle. Perhaps we should not back it. Perhaps, simply because it has slept for so long, we should be foolish not to back it. All right—let's back both; we have something in hand from our previous success.

Final 7 wins immediately, showing a profit of 33 units. We could of course hedge here, balancing the loss from Final 0, now up to 40 units, against our present profit from all the columns—79 units. We adventure, and continue with the series. It still loses—another 36 units gone.

This, we must point out, was not the way the hard grafter would have played. He had a chance to hedge and show a nice profit. He takes those chances. Nevertheless, even with this setback, the gambler would by no means flinch and retire. With no Final 0 showing in two complete columns he would assuredly continue to back it with a progression, using his third series, 2 units. (Although, being the gambler, he would probably have used a second series of 2 units and now be using either 3 units or 4 units.) He would achieve success on the fourth spin. So whether we use his method or that of the hard grafter we come out of this little adventure very satisfactorily.

Notation

The simplest method of notation is to write the numbers as they win. There is plenty of room in the margins of the standard record card.

Draw a line across the numbers columns nine spins from the bottom to show when we have reached Spin No. 28. If a number has not yet been written down its omission will be obvious to the eye and will indicate the target. Having backed it, fill it in. For the next line simply cross the numbers off as they win, when any number not crossed off at Spin No. 28 will again indicate the target.

Dozens

A popular method of play, especially among players who play high or fairly high, is to back two dozens, giving odds of 2–1. The basic idea is to snatch a quick win of a set amount. With two dozens favourable and only one against the chances are that an early profit will be obtained. Should this be sufficient, play is stopped at once. Over an extended period however the Zero effect should swing the balance in favour of the House. Nevertheless many excellent results have been obtained by the method in spite of the fact that it is almost always incorrectly employed.

The standard (incorrect) procedure is to place the stake across the first and second or second and third dozens, playing to win one unit. The first and third dozens may be backed by placing a stake on each, there being no line of junction between these.

When the Zero wins all stakes are of course lost, and this is where the error in placement arises. It is unusual because of the very small gain to use minimum stakes on these bets. So the stake used is almost always divisible by four. This is of sufficient size to enable correct play to be made.

Drill

Taking the stake to be divisible by four, call it 4 units; place 3 units on the relevant even chance, i.e. Manque (Low) if the first and second dozens are being backed, Passe (High) if the second and third dozens are being backed. The other unit is placed on the Sixain adjacent to this, i.e. 19–24 should Manque have been backed, 13–18 should Passe have been backed.

Now, should Zero win, three-quarters of the stake is merely imprisoned, not lost; may lose, may win, may be shared if so desired. On balance only half of this is lost, which gives a direct saving of stake of three-eights, $37\frac{1}{2}\%$. Thus incorrect play after a number of plays amounting to a total stake of a hundred pounds, is subject to an average loss to Zero of two pounds fourteen shillings. Playing correctly, this is reduced to one pound fourteen shillings.

This does not sound a lot but over a period it is important, especially if the stake be high. A high player may stake forty pounds a spin with this kind of play. Playing for three hours at an American table (or the equivalent of three hours over a period), he must expect to see the Zero win about nine times. Correct play will therefore on average save him the sum of £135. A player staking £4 per spin will save £13–10–0. This is not inconsiderable for a little trouble taken to use better technique.

Progression on Two Dozens

This requires an extremely quick rise of stake so should not be undertaken until the hypothetical bet position is suitable. This means that the third dozen, the one not being backed, must have won a certain number of times in succession. How many?

The odds against any dozen are 2–1. As we use four hypothetical bets for even chances, it appears that for the alien dozen to win twice in succession should be adequate. This, however, is slightly risky because of the lack of length unavoidable in our progression, so it is recommended that the play not be undertaken until that dozen has won three times in succession.

Drill (Backing 1st and 2nd dozens)

Place 3 units on Manque, 1 unit on the sixain 19–24. This loses. Second bet: 9 units on Manque; 3 units on 19–24. If lost: 27 units on Manque. 9 units on 19–26. This is as far as such a progression should go unless a large capital is available. The next would be 81 on Manque, 27 on 19–24, a stake of 108 units.

In practice it is rare for a particular dozen, 2–1 against, to win as many as six times running. However, should the bet be fancied, an extra hypothetical bet may be employed, using the play not as a regular one but merely an adjunct to normal play, a small profit to be picked up by the way.

Recording the Dozens

Dozens can of course be read by the experienced player glancing down his columns of numbers. Should difficulty be experienced a simple Union Jack method may be used, employing one of the columns normally used for figures.

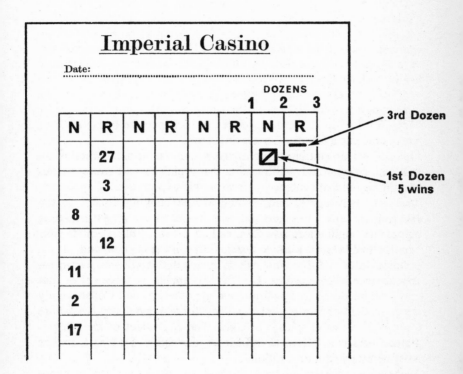

The fourth column has been reserved for notation of dozens. No. 27 wins; a line is drawn horizontally in the last third of the two columns combined. No. 3 wins; a similar line is drawn in the first third. No. 8 wins; a perpendicular line is joined to the previous one in the first column. No. 12 wins. Another perpendicular is added. No. 11 wins. A fourth line goes in the 'first dozen' column, this time horizontal, and completing a square. No. 2 wins, still the first dozen, so a diagonal line is drawn across the completed square. The first dozen has therefore won five times running, and a progression on the other two seems to be a fair bet.

The Single Dozen

'As odds against the single dozen are 2–1, an adverse run against it may theoretically be twice as long as one against an even chance position. Therefore, as we recommended four hypothetical bets to be used for a complete progression against an even chance it seems fair enough to allot eight with the single dozen. Should a particular dozen fail to win in eight successive spins it may be backed with a reasonable expectation of appearing soon.'

This is typical gaming-book analysis and, as usual, contains an optical illusion which will deceive many players and cause serious loss. With the last sentence—a reasonable expectation of appearing soon—we may agree, and, should we be backing dozens to the exclusion of any other method, we would be backing them long before that eight successive failures had shown. But to equate four hypothetical bets for a single dozen with eight spins is wrong.

A single dozen is 2–1 against, which means that it will—on average— appear once in three spins. If it fails to appear in three spins, that may be considered to constitute one hypothetical bet. Consequently the equivalent of four hypothetical bets for a single dozen is a failure to appear in *twelve* spins, not eight. The equivalent of *three* hypothetical bets is a failure to appear in nine spins. Dozens therefore must be attacked with caution.

A complete progression on a single dozen would be: (three hypothetical bets used)

0 0 0 0 0 0 0 0 0 1 1 2 3 4 6 9 13 20 30 45 68 102 etc.

The stake of 13 units at positive bet No. 8 is an insurance bet.

This looks like a very long progression, practically guaranteeing immunity from loss. It isn't. It holds 22 bets, the equivalent of an 11-bet progression against an even chance position. We do not recommend complete progressions against even chances with so few bets, so we do not recommend this either.

The capital requirement for the progression as it stands is 304 units. To make the progression long enough to equate a 13-timer on an even chance would require four more bets, respectively 153, 229, 344 and 516 units, a total capital requirement of 1,546 units.

Time Factor

This practically rules out the use of complete progressions on the single dozen as a basic method. By strict arithmetic we may expect a dozen to fail to appear nine or twelve times, as frequently as an even chance position fails to appear three or four times, but it will still take three times as long at the table.

It is therefore recommended that the play on single dozens be used purely as an ancillary method, subservient to the standard play. Because of this subservience and its periodical impact upon the manual routine, it is also advisable that the drill be kept simple, which means that staking-plans must be short.

If capital admits, a six-bet sequence is reasonable. This is the beginning of the above line, i.e. 1 1 2 3 4 6 needing 17 units in all and giving a profit for each respective win of: 2, 1, 2, 2, 1 and 1 units. It is reasonable to include insurance betting with:

One insurance bet, (No. 3)	1 1 1 2 3 5 7
Two, (Nos. 3 and 6)	1 1 1 2 3 4 7
Three, (Nos. 3, 6 and 7)	1 1 1 2 3 4 6

An under-insurance line may be used, comparable to a Split Martingale line: 1 1 1 2 2 3 3 4 5 6 if conservation of capital is the major factor.

An abbreviated series of Split Martingale lines may also be used, as

Line 1. 1 1 *1* insurance;	or	1 1 2 normal.	
Line 2. 2 2 *2*	„	2 2 3	„
Line 3. 3 3 *3*	„	3 3 4	„

This is reasonable play and is likely to be suitable of it is desired to concentrate upon dozens as the basic method.

Bread and Butter

This type of line accepts a limited loss, so should be Lines 1 and 2 as above, either with or without insurance according to preference.

If all six bets lose the essay is abandoned, the loss accepted and a fresh series started.

With slightly more freedom of capital the series may be permitted to escalate slowly. Use Lines 1 and 2. If they fail, accept the loss but recommence with Line 2 and follow with Line 3. Immediate wins may quickly clear the previous, accepted loss, when the line should revert to Line 1.

Staccato progression on Single Dozens

A recommended method; one however which requires control and perhaps some extra book-keeping. It is ancillary to normal methods and may sometimes have to be carried forward from session to session of play.

Drill

When the first or third dozen (NOT the second) has won three successive coups;

1st Doz.: Stake 3 units on Passe; 1 unit on the Sixain 13–18.
3rd Doz.: Stake 3 units on Manque; 1 unit on the sixain 19–24.

Result, if successful, is a win of 2 units whether the even chance or the adjacent sixain wins.
One bet only is made.
Should it fail a note is made of the loss, i.e. 4 units, and a progression on the position is started, playing one bet only each time the qualifying dozens produce three consecutive wins.

The progression should be basically in the form of a Split, not a complete Martingale, although certain bets may clear the line entirely. Fundamental arithmetic tells us that the bet is 2–1 in our favour, so the amount of gain desired from the average bet in the progression should be some 5–2 in our favour against the outstanding line. This naturally demands a certain amount of capital but should clear the line more quickly than it builds up.

Suitable progression

The loss is 4 units. With a win of 2 units, two bets clear one loss. Requiring some 5–2 against 4 units we need a bet which will produce a gain of—in these circumstances—3 units. Now each win will do more than its automatic work so should clear the line at reasonable speed.

For perfect smoothness of progression the initial placements should be abandoned. The stakes may be placed on the opposite end dozen plus the relevant two sixains, or, alternatively, on the relevant four sixains.

Thus: the first dozen wins three times running. We stake 3 units on Passe and 1 unit on the sixain 13–18. The first dozen however wins once more, and the loss is 4 units.

Drill for recovery

Bet No.	Position	
	Opposite doz. (top)	Sixains 13–18; 19–24 each
1	4 units	2 units
2	6	3
3	8	4

This is an under insurance series because to inaugurate a complete progression would take the stake extremely high. It would need:

1	4 units	2 units
2	12	6
3	36	18

If all bets fail, the loss with the first series is 36 units, plus of course the 4 units we are attempting to recover. With the second series it is 104 units plus 4.

This type of progression is all very well if capital is plentiful, but normally the sensible way seems to be to accept the loss of 4 units, either by writing it off, or by gradual recovery.

Using the four sixains as opposed to the opposite dozen and two sixains, the series is:

1	1 unit on each of the four sixains.
2	3 units
3	9 units

This already seems plenty of units to use for a recovery of a mere 4 units. Not only so, but this series wins only 2 units per success. Success is more than likely, of course; it is almost sure; but that 'almost' still inclines us to eschew the risk.

Final judgment

After reviewing the possibilities, the best way to handle this bet—a good one we must emphasise, which is why we take the trouble to analyse the possible continuations—is to accept the loss of 4 units, keep the record on a separate page in the p & l ledger, and see how it goes after a period. We venture to suggest that by the time we are due to declare a dividend, there will be something in the kitty which will make this possible.

Once the bet is found to be profitable in the long run it will quite naturally be incorporated into the standard procedure of the player and duly recognised whenever the opportunity for its use occurs.

The Middle Dozen

There being no even chance covering 18 numbers to use against the middle dozen, in similar circumstances, should the play be desired, the stakes must be placed on the other two dozens and the occasional loss through Zero accepted.

Flat stake on Single Dozen

An ancillary method emerging naturally from the examination of the compression of first dozen numbers into a block, p. 205, and based upon the rhythm theory.

Drill

The 'block' numbers are, in arithmetical sequence:

$$5 \quad 6 \quad 8 \quad 10 \quad 11 \qquad 13 \quad 23 \quad 27 \quad 30 \quad 36$$

When any of the last five numbers shows, back the first dozen for 1 unit and for four successive plays.

Continue with the same stake if further numbers from the block appear. The results of this method are only felt over a period, but experience tells that about 1 unit per column should accrue in the overall balance-sheet.

Example of Drill

Numbers win in sequence:

30	This is from the block. Prepare to stake 1 unit four times.
34	
28	
3	First dozen wins, clearing the previous two losses.
27	First dozen fails but produces another number from the block, suggesting that the rhythm is still there. Play four more numbers, still at 1 unit stake.
28	
2	Clears the previous two losses.
13	Another number from the block.
9	Win of 1 unit is registered. This however is not only the fourth play engendered by No. 27, but also the first play engendered by No. 13. *Three* more plays are therefore indicated, not four.
14	
12	Wins
33	Last play. No fresh number from the block has appeared. Actual winning targets as would be, for example, the first five numbers in the block, should not be considered as demanding a continuation of play. 1 unit is the total profit here. That is as much as we should expect. Over a period the addition of this sort of play will make a noticeable difference to our overall tally. No increase of stake is ever made, even though a lengthy line of loss builds up.

Repetition of Single Dozens

A useful ancillary method based upon a pattern principle.

Drill

Wait until a dozen has repeated itself in successive spins. Wait further until a change in the dozen comes. Back the new dozen for

1 unit. If it wins, stop. Wait until a fresh repeat shows and carry out the same drill.

If it loses continue with two more bets, still of 1 unit, backing each time the immediate dominant, the dozen which last won, playing for a repeat.

Progression

When the loss line reaches six, 1 1 1 1 1 1 increase the stake to 2 units. When the loss line reaches 1 1 1 1 1 1 2 2 2 2 2 2 increase to 4 units. If the loss line reaches to 1 1 1 1 1 1 2 2 2 2 2 2 4 4 4 4 4 4 increase to 8 units. Total capital 90 units.

It is advisable to use the capital to its full value in this type of progression, avoiding insurance bets or gradual progressions. The immediate necessity is to clear the line quickly and this is a prior consideration to safety. Safe play will probably cause the loss line to remain fairly low but indefinitely uncleared.

This ancillary method is recommended. The account should be kept separately as is the Zero account, the amount of any outstanding line carried forward from session to session, each time commencing the line where it left off.

Profitable ancillary plays to include dozens

For these attractive plays we must often discard the technique demanded previously of splitting our stake on two dozens between an even chance and a sixain. The margin of the Zero is accepted.

Series 1

When numbers have won twice in succession in the same transversal: (1, 3; 17, 18, etc., but NOT 18, 19). e.g. Two numbers win, Nos. 8 and 7. They are from the same transversal, 7, 8, 9.

Place 4 units on each of the second and third dozens; 1 unit on the transversal 10, 11, 12; 2 units on the sixain 1–6. (Or 1 unit on each of its transversals—it is immaterial which.)

This covers 33 numbers and wins 1 unit except against Zero or a third win for the 7, 8, 9 transversal.

Technique

With this particular sequence which allots 4 units to the dozens, the standard technique of splitting the stake may be used, placing 6 units on (here) Passe and 2 units on the sixain 13–18.

Knowledge

From this it becomes apparent that familiarity with routine is important. The player without serious experience is likely to get thoroughly muddled with this type of play. It is better for him to take his chance of Zero winning until he has his manual drill at his finger-tips, knows automatically the number of units required for each position and can place his bets swiftly and efficiently without interfering with his standard system.

Series 2

When a particular sixain has won three times in succession, say the sixain 1–6 with perhaps Nos. 6, 2 and 4: Stake 2 units on the second and third dozens, 1 unit on the sixain 7–12. Total stake 5 units; wins 1 unit unless Zero or the 1–6 sixain wins once more. Covers 30 numbers.

Here, should it be desired to take advantage of the standard technique, the stake must be doubled, using 4 units for each dozen, but placing 6 units on (here) Passe, 2 units on the sixain 13–18 and 2 units on the sixain 7–12. This, of course, shows a profit of 2 units should it win.

Series 2a

The previous Series 2 showed an 'end' sixain winning three times running, i.e. a sixain comprising the six numbers either first in a particular dozen or last. The one exampled, 1–6, comprised the first six numbers in the first dozen. The sixain 7–12 is also an 'end' sixain, comprising the last six numbers in the same dozen.

A 'middle' sixain here would be 4–9, the six middle numbers of the first dozen, and this of course will necessitate a different placement of stake, there being no sixain available.

Example: Nos. 30, 33 and 28 win in succession. These are all from the 'middle' sixain in the top dozen. Our bet is therefore upon the 30 numbers outside that sixain. This must include 1 unit each on the transversals 25–27 and 34–36 plus stakes upon the first and second dozens.

A stake of 2 units on each of these dozens would give a win of 4 units for a winning dozen, but this is not enough, as the other dozen and the two transversals lose 4 units. It equates an insurance bet on dozens with concentration upon the possibility of a win for one of the transversals which would provide a gain of 6 units in such circumstances. But such concentration is patently vulnerable to the threat of Zero to lose the total stakes of 6 units once for every six wins (on rough average). This sends the percentage advantage of the Zero to a level which we certainly should not tolerate.

The stake on the dozens must accordingly be adjusted to provide a win rather than simple insurance. We could use 3 units on each dozen, providing a gain of 6 units against a loss of 5 units, profit 1 unit. (Loss is 3 units on the other dozen and 1 unit on each of the transversals.)

This, however, still puts strain on the transversals, forcing them to give a profit of 4 units once in (roughly) six attempts, again open to the threat of Zero, instead of taking a 2 units profit every spin of the wheel in such positions. The load is better spread more evenly, staking 4 units for each dozen against the same 1 unit for each transversal.

Once this is done we may employ the standard splitting technique, automatically saving three-eighths of our total stake whenever Zero wins; losing 5 units instead of 8 units, an important consideration over an extended period.

The stakes will therefore be against the treble win of the 'middle' sixain of the last dozen, Nos. 30, 33 and 28:

6 units on Manque.
2 units on the sixain 19–24.
1 unit on each of the transversals 25–27 and 34–36.

Series 3
When one particular dozen has won four times in succession, say the first.

Stake 1 unit on each of the other dozens, here the second and the third. This gives 1 unit profit if either dozen wins.

Advantage may be taken of the standard technique for splitting the stake if 4 units are used instead of 1 unit. Stake 6 units on (here) Passe, 2 units on the sixain 13–18. This produces a win of 4 units if successful, the quadrupled stake naturally showing four times the gain.

This is not recommended unless the unit used is capable of division by four. Thus if the minimum stake is 5/– the single unit play may be used if the player's own unit is of one pound, staking 15/– on the even chance, 5/– on the sixain. This smacks of one law for the rich and another for the poor. It is. The poor man must take his chance of Zero; the rich man has the advantage of the standard splitting technique.

Nevertheless, there is no reason why this type of bet should not be subjected to a progression. The bet loses. Wait again until a particular dozen has won four times running. Now stake an insurance bet of 2 units on each of the other dozens.

It is advisable to use insurance here because when backing two positions *in combination* a progression mounts at fearsome speed. To show an immediate profit the line is:

$$1 \quad 3 \quad 9 \quad 27 \quad 81$$
$$1 \quad 3 \quad 9 \quad 27 \quad 81$$

An under-insurance line is therefore strongly to be advised, as
1 1 (under-insurance) 2 (under-insurance) 3 (under-insurance) 4
1 1   2   3   4
(under-insurance)
This type of line will, of course, clear the previous loss very gradually but it will avoid the disaster which can so easily strike if a complete progression is undertaken.

Series 4

When one particular column has won four times in succession, back the other columns for 1 unit each. There is of course no technical splitting advantage available as is sometimes there with dozens, and this must be accepted.

The position with regard to progressions is precisely the same as immediately above with Series 3. The under-insurance line is the one to play unless capital is plentiful.

Overall

This collection of ancillary plays must be recommended. Familiarity with routine is important; familiarity with the record card is essential; the player must be able to glance at his card and appreciate when this type of bet is available, whether the last four spins have shown four successive wins for one dozen or one column, whether the last three have shown three for one sixain, whether the last two have shown two for one transversal. And he must not get mixed up about what is actually in, especially, sixains and transversals. Nos. 18, 20 and 22 are not in the same sixain; Nos. 12, 13 and 14 are not in the same transversal.

Roulette is a game of skill. To play it well and profitably that skill must be acquired. Plugging away with a good system is all very well but without the ability to change it will eventually lead to disaster; without the knowledge which enables us to recognise the numerous extremely favourable positions which continually present themselves, our overall gains will be seriously less than they should be.

This plethora of differing stakes on various positions must inevitably be viewed as something of a headache by the inexperienced player. He can, however, do plenty to assist himself by careful preparation. Here is an example of a record card which he may prepare in advance and refer to whenever a suitable position arrives:

	Hypo.	E.C.	D.D.		C.C.		Six.	Trans.		
Trans	2	6					2	1	1	1
End Six.	3		2	2			1			
Mid. Six.	3		2	2				1	1	
Col.	4				1	1				
Doz.	4		1	1						

Reads: *Trans.* = a position for a bet on a transversal is available when *Hypo.* one transversal has won twice running. The stakes are:

E.C. 6 units on the relevant even chance.

Six. 2 units on the adjacent sixain.

Trans. 1 unit each on the remaining three transversals.

A record like this will fit quite comfortably into the space available on the back of a visiting card, easy to read and unobtrusive.

There are plentiful opportunities for the preparation of similar reference-cards for any desired situation, and the serious player will not be ashamed to use them to the full.

The Split Martingale

The simple Martingale system is the doubling-up line we have seen. It endeavours to win 1 unit each time and stakes the entire capital upon success.

The Split Martingale sets out to win one-third of the bets made, clearing off two losses by each win. This seems to be a far more modest ambition and less likely to lead to disaster when the adverse run or preponderance comes.

We will examine it, see what its advantages are and also discover what is wrong with it. It is probably the most popular system ever devised, and has been used for many years by thousands of optimistic punters. It usually wins too, but it is dangerous, and the danger it courts is only appreciated after serious analysis or extended experience at the table.

There are many possible lines to use, but one of the most common is the 1 2 3 4 5 line. This is the drill: These figures are written down and a bet of 1 unit is placed upon a chosen position. For the moment we will stick to our original choice, and back no other position.

If the bet wins the gain is pocketed and the line stays unchanged. When the first loss is incurred, it is written at the end of the line, thus: 1 2 3 4 5 1. The next stake is the sum of the two outside figures, i.e. 2 units.

After each win thenceforward the two outside figures are crossed off, as: 1 2 3 4 5 1. Again the next stake is the sum of the two outside figures, now 7 units. Every win will cancel two figures, every loss add only one. Two losses are therefore cancelled by each win, and to win one-third of the bets made should be enough to win consistently. We check the truth of this shortly. When the last figure is cleared off, the line now blank, the total of the original figures has been won. We started with 1 2 3 4 5—total 15 units. We added only our own losses. When the line is clear, we have cleared all our losses plus the original line, so have won 15 units more than we lost. Here is the method in action. We back RED.

Bet No.	Stake	Col. wins	Win	Lose	Line (starts 1 2 3 4 5)
1	1	R	1		1 2 3 4 5
2	1	B		1	1 2 3 4 5 1
3	2	R	2		2 3 4 5
4	7	R	7		3 4
5	7	R	7		1 2 3 4 5 (16 units won)
6	1	B		1	1 2 3 4 5 1
7	2	B		2	1 2 3 4 5 1 2
8	3	B		3	1 2 3 4 5 1 2 3
9	4	R	4		2 3 4 5 1 2 3
10	5	B		5	2 3 4 5 1 2 5
11	7	R	7		3 4 5 1 2
12	5	R	5		4 5 1
13	5	B		5	4 5 1 5
14	9	R	9		5 1
15	6	R	6		1 2 3 4 5 (15 units won)

Two series have been cleared, showing a profit of 31 units, 1 unit having been won without having to change the line.

We take the same series of numbers and back BLACK instead of Red.

Bet No.	Stake	Col. wins	Win	Lose	Line (starts 1 2 3 4 5)
1	1	R		1	1 2 3 4 5 1
2	2	B	2		2 3 4 5
3	7	R		7	2 3 4 5 7
4	9	R		9	2 3 4 5 7 9
5	11	R		11	2 3 4 5 7 9 11
6	13	B	13		3 4 5 7 9
7	12	B	12		4 5 7
8	11	B	11		5

At this stage, having gone to as high a stake as 13 units and having had three good wins in a row, caution would suggest that this remaining 5 units be written off, contenting ourselves with a profit of 10 units and starting a fresh line. We will however continue as we are for purposes of comparison.

Bet No.	Stake	Col. wins	Win	Lose	Line (starts 1 2 3 4 5)
9	5	R		5	5 5
10	10	B	10		1 2 3 4 5

Caution would have been wrong that time.

Bet No.	Stake	Col. wins	Win	Lose	Line (starts 1 2 3 4 5)
11	1	R		1	1 2 3 4 5 1
12	2	R		2	1 2 3 4 5 1 2
13	3	B	3		2 3 4 5 1
14	3	R		3	2 3 4 5 1 3
15	5	R		5	2 3 4 5 1 3 5

What happens now we cannot tell, although we note that Red has an advantage of nine wins against six, a pretty good score, hardly an average, actually a 50% advantage. With reasonable distribution of Fortune's favours however this line should clear itself with not too much trouble. All that is needed is three or four quick wins, or, alternately, eight out of the next seventeen, less than half. It does not seem too much to require.

This Split Martingale is therefore arithmetically sound. The only points to be checked now are (a) can it remain below the House maximum? and (b) will it over-extend the available capital? If it answers those two questions satisfactorily we may consider it 100%. The answer is of course foregone: it isn't. Were it so, every casino would have gone out of business years ago. Here is a series which includes a strong preponderance for the position we did not choose. We chose RED.

Bet No.	Stake	Col. wins	Win	Lose	Line (starts 1 2 3 4 5)
1	1	B		1	1 2 3 4 5 1
2	2	R	2		2 3 4 5
3	7	R	7		3 4
4	7	B		7	3 4 7
5	10	B		10	3 4 7 10
6	13	B		13	3 4 7 10 13
7	16	B		16	3 4 7 10 13 16
8	19	B		19	3 4 7 10 13 16 19
9	22	B		22	3 4 7 10 13 16 19 22
10	25	B		25	3 4 7 10 13 16 19 22 25
11	28	B		28	3 4 7 10 13 16 19 22 25 28
12	31	R	31		4 7 10 13 16 19 22 25
13	29	B		29	4 7 10 13 16 19 22 25 29
14	33	R	33		7 10 13 16 19 22 25
15	32	R	32		10 13 16 19 22
16	32	B		32	10 13 16 19 22 32
17	42	B		42	10 13 16 19 22 32 42
18	52	B		52	10 13 16 19 22 32 42 52
19	62	B		62	10 13 16 19 22 32 42 52 62
20	72	R	72		13 16 19 22 32 42 52
21	65	B		65	13 16 19 22 32 42 52 65
22	78	R	78		16 19 22 32 42 52
23	68	R	68		19 22 32 42
24	61	B		61	19 22 32 42 61

A capital of 340 units is required in this series up to now. This is not overlarge compared with the type of capital we have seen in single progressions, where the final bet by itself may require 192 units.

Yet we must, having seen this, consider not merely what has happened but what might happen, for that is the eternal problem at the Roulette table. Black has won sixteen out of 24 spins here, but a Roulette wheel has no memory; it has no personal interest in producing averages, so is quite capable of persisting with a preponderance for Black. Not for ever of course, but 'for ever' is not our concern; our concern is the next few spins. Should these produce another half-dozen Blacks, the line would require a capital of 941 units with a stake yet to be placed of 194 units, thus making a total capital of 941 + 194 — 15 (the original line) = 1120 units.

And this is far removed from what may eventually arrive. This sort of line can depass the thousand mark in units of stake. Obviously, therefore, it is dangerous occasionally. The trouble is that 'occasionally' may not sound often but when it arrives it spells disaster, something not to be welcomed even occasionally. Once is usually more than enough.

Clearly something must be amended, and we suggest initially that the line is too ambitious; that we should not set ourselves the task of winning 7 units almost at once; and that a line 1 1 1 1 1 would be far less likely to leap into the hundred-unit stakes so swiftly. For thirty spins does not take long at an American table, maybe twenty minutes. If disaster arrives at an early stage it will seem to hit us before we have really settled in to play. We examine therefore the 1 1 1 1 1 line using this same sequence of 24 spins. Still backing RED.

Bet No.	Stake	Col. Wins	Win	Lose	Line (starts 1 1 1 1 1)								
1	1	B		1	1	1	1	1	1	1			
2	2	R	2		1	1	1	1					
3	2	R	2		1	1							
4	2	B		2	1	1	2						
5	3	B		3	1	1	2	3					
6	4	B		4	1	1	2	3	4				
7	5	B		5	1	1	2	3	4	5			
8	6	B		6	1	1	2	3	4	5	6		
9	7	B		7	1	1	2	3	4	5	6	7	
10	8	B		8	1	1	2	3	4	5	6	7	8
11	9	B		9	1	1	2	3	4	5	6	7	8	9
12	10	R	10		1	2	3	4	5	6	7	8	
13	9	B	9		1	2	3	4	5	6	7	8	9
14	10	R	10		2	3	4	5	6	7	8		
15	10	R	10		3	4	5	6	7				

Bet No.	Stake	Col. Wins	Win	Lose	Line (starts 1 1 1 1 1)
16	10	B		10	3 4 5 6 7 10
17	13	B		13	3 4 5 6 7 10 13
18	16	B		16	3 4 5 6 7 10 13 16
19	19	B		19	3 4 5 6 7 10 13 16 19
20	22	R	22		4 5 6 7 10 13 16
21	20	B		20	4 5 6 7 10 13 16 20
22	24	R	24		5 6 7 10 13 16
23	21	R	21		6 7 10 13
24	19	B		19	6 7 10 13 19

Deducting the 5 units with which the original line started, we are at present losing 50 units. In the 1 2 3 4 5 line, using the same results, we were losing 160 units. This simple line 1 1 1 1 1 is therefore seen not only to be capable of keeping our capital requirements much lower, keeping us in the game much longer, but also of staying below the House maximum more easily.

Illusion

Fired with an enthusiasm to keep the stake low, the early analyst will assuredly at this stage get the idea that to have a permanent figure of 1 unit at the commencement of the line would automatically prevent the stake from leaping up as it does when the first figure starts to get large.

This does not work. The basic idea—not accurate as we shall see shortly—is to clear two losses by each win. To have a permanent unit of 1 at the beginning of the line, replacing it the moment it was wiped off would simply be converting the entire system from a Martingale to an Alembert. Doing that we would have to win once for every time we lost in order to clear the line.

We could then lengthen the line? 1 1 1 1 1 1 1 perhaps? But this has the same effect even if it is only temporary. It is in fact using the 1 1 1 1 1 line but putting an extra 1 unit in front of it after each of the first two wins, making the system a true Alembert until all the single units have been cleared.

Even our 1 1 1 1 1 line is actually doing precisely that, and the true Split Martingale is only reached when we reduce that line to a single figure of 1 unit. Here we examine the basic flaw in the Split Martingale method.

Split Martingale Analysis

The initial hope is to cancel two losses by each win, thus needing (disregarding the Zero effect) to win only one-third of our bets in order to beat the table.

The inherent flaw in the theory is that it fails to do just this. One reason is of course the Zero effect. Another is the wasted win. Thus, having written down our chosen line we win our first bet. This has not cancelled two losses; it has not cancelled any loss, so, if we win merely one-third of our bets and these are to cancel all the losses the equation fails to equate; we shall need one win more than one-third once we have wasted that first win. To have won that will mean that there will be two bets uncancelled at the close, and these may be quite large figures. If we start with half-a-dozen straight wins we shall obviously require a still greater proportion.

But even this does not reveal the built-in inefficiency of the drill. Line 1 1 1 1 1. First bet lost. Line is 1 1 1 1 1 1. To clear this we need three wins. But if we get them we have not cancelled two losses by each win but have actually taken three wins to clear one single loss. The basic ambition of the method is immediately penalised for a false start and has to start some yards behind the scratch mark.

The answer is that we have deliberately handicapped ourselves by writing down a line at all. Clearing one loss by one win is something we cannot avoid if only one loss has been made. Winning some bets before we start to lose is something else we cannot avoid—even if we wanted to. To have to use up our precious winners in these ways is unavoidable, but to have to use them to cancel losses that do not actually exist is hardly efficient, especially as the practice increases the amount of stake and so makes inroads upon our capital.

One sensible solution must clearly be to write down nothing to begin with. To write a figure only after it has been lost. Now if a line develops we may be sure that each winning coup writes off two losing ones, there being no phony losses in our record.

The drill must therefore be to stake 1 unit over and above the sum of the two outside figures if a profit is desired. Thus:

Lose 1 unit. Line is: 1		Stake 2 units
Lose	1 2	Stake 4
Lose	1 2 4	Stake 6
Lose	1 2 4 6	Stake 8

The two outside figures are added and to their sum is mentally added 1 unit as profit. The first three figures—1 2 4—are unavoidably identical with the complete Martingale line but the stake diminishes sharply afterwards. Eight consecutive losses with this type of line would produce 1 2 4 6 8 10 12 14 against the complete Martingale line of 1 2 4 8 16 32 64 128.

We replay the last series of 24 spins using this method of writing nothing but concrete losses.

Bet No.	Stake	Col. wins	Win	Lose	Line (starts at nil)							
1	1	B		1	1							
2	2	R	2		clear							
3	1	R	1		clear							
4	1	B		1	1							
5	2	B		2	1	2						
6	4	B		4	1	2	4					
7	6	B		6	1	2	4	6				
8	8	B		8	1	2	4	6	8			
9	10	B		10	1	2	4	6	8	10		
10	12	B		12	1	2	4	6	8	10	12	
11	14	B		14	1	2	4	6	8	10	12	14
12	16	R	16		2	4	6	8	10	12		
13	15	B		15	2	4	6	8	10	12	15	
14	18	R	18		4	6	8	10	12			
15	17	R	17		6	8	10					
16	17	B		17	6	8	10	17				
17	24	B		24	6	8	10	17	24			
18	31	B		31	6	8	10	17	24	31		
19	38	B		38	6	8	10	17	24	31	38	
20	45	R	45		8	10	17	24	31			
21	40	B		40	8	10	17	24	31	40		
22	49	R	49		10	17	24	31				
23	42	R	42		17	24						
24	42	B		42	17	24	42					

This produces a final line of 83 units. This is more than the previous 1 1 1 1 1 required with its final line of 6 7 10 13 19 = 55 units, which is understandable, for, as we have seen, that line is actually a semi-Alembert, succeeding for a long time in cancelling only one loss by each win. The 1 2 3 4 5 line finished 19 22 25 35 54 = 155. The basic advantage is seen in the number of figures remaining in the line—five in the two previous methods, only three with this one. On our final spin, therefore, we merely had to produce one win instead of one loss to clear the line entirely.

This method therefore, of writing down only genuine losses, has a much better chance to keep the line clear than either of the others. Nevertheless it can also start to climb into the stratosphere of stake-level and so should be employed with circumspection.

The most efficient drill is to write a line of hypothetical loss consisting of a single unit: 1. When we wrote nothing we had to lose twice before a win cancelled two losses. Therefore if we write in one imaginary loss we do not affect the principle of the Split Martingale in any way. At the same time we can reduce our overall rise of stake. No mental addition is now required—the addition is written down for us already.

The line starts: 1. One win of 1 unit clears it, and it is rewritten. (In practice of course it will simply be left as it is unless the record is desired to show the precise amount of gain.) If the first coup is lost, the line will be: 1 1 and the next stake be the standard addition of the two outside figures, i.e. 2. The line now mounts in single units until a win is achieved, four straight losses producing 1 2 3 4 to be cleared by two wins of 5 units each.

Each time the line is cleared a profit of 1 unit is made. This is modest compared with the ambitious 15-unit line with which we started but it is more than adequate for the hard grafter. Enormous profits are made by courting enormous losses. Once he has avoided losing, finishing his session with his line clear or almost clear, he may scrutinise his record and will there find, dotted about, a scattering of ticks which constitute wins. These, added up, will give a very acceptable total.

Once a player can do this he is on the high road to consistent success. The number of wins is not important; to win more it is merely necessary to play in exactly the same way with a higher stake. Having learned to control the game, the hard grafter will be able to afford that stake and may soon find himself playing for pounds instead of for shillings.

The Moving Target

The Split Martingale, hitherto seen on a set target, may of course be used on a changing target, as against all twelve of the inherent even chance positions we have listed. Here is a constructed column. Four hypothetical bets are used.

Split Martingale staking-plan. Line starts: *1*.

(N)	(R)		
B	R		
	19		
	12		
	3		
	34	1 unit on Black.	
8		Wins. No bet here.	*1 1*
	24	No bet.	
17		Four-time High-Low alternation. Back the dominant. 1 unit Low.	
	3	Wins. Four-time colour alternation. Back the dominant. 1 unit Red.	*1 1* 1
	18	Wins. No bet here.	*1 1 1 1*
10		Four Low. 1 unit High.	
29		Wins. No bet here.	*1 1 1 1 1*
	9	Double dominant, two Red, two Black in isolation. Bet against the continuation. 1 unit Black.	
	7	Loses. 2 units against it remaining a double dominant. 2 units Red.	*1 1 1 1 1* 1
22		Loses. 3 units Red against it becoming another double.	*1 1 1 1 1* 1 2
	34	Wins.	*1 1 1 1 1*

The line is clear except for the hypothetical bet. 4 units have been won.

Reading the Record card

This is obviously important. The inexperienced player would probably have missed more than one available bet in this series. Harking back to the previous section on Ancillary Plays to include Dozens, we note that the wins for Nos. 9 and 7 are from the same transversal, so a play on 33 numbers is indicated.

In addition, the final three numbers, Nos. 7, 22 and 34 are all from the first column. One more in that column will make another bet available—on the other two columns. The player prepared to take a greater 'risk' on a purely ancillary bet may bet on them now.

Good bets are continually missed by most players. To be able to read the record card efficiently is financially extremely beneficial, and deserves some study.

Reduction of the Split Martingale Line

The Split Martingale, setting out to win (in theory) one bet to clear two losses, initially requires far less capital than does the natural Martingale, i.e. double-up line. In a 10-bet series these compare:

Double-up:	1	2	4	8	16	32	64	128	256	512
Split:		1	2	4	6	8	10	12	14	16	18

This looks like an enormous capital reduction. Unfortunately it may be temporary, for while the double-up line inevitably dies at the tenth bet, the Split line can go on indefinitely, and may be of twenty or even thirty-bet length should the adverse preponderance become really serious. Not only so, but, once the series contains a number of wins, the small figures at the beginning have been wiped out, and the line now forces the stake to rise by leaps and bounds. Clear five wins from that line within a series of losses and the first figure becomes 10 units. Every successive bet must then increase by that number. Soon enough the line may read something like 28 46 64 82 110 and, a couple of spins later, one win, one loss, read 46 64 82 128 with the next stake to be 174 units.

This is somewhat frightening, so if we can make some reduction it should relieve the financial pressure if not the psychological.

We start with the assumption that we desire—more or less—to clear two losses by each win, and our basic line is to commence with one hypothetical loss of 1 unit. The first three figures will be 1 1 2. To clear two losses the next figure must be 3. Losing, the line becomes 1 1 2 3. (Six units lost, the first figure being hypothetical.) Basically the Split Martingale now requires a bet of 4 units. Can this be reduced? Not yet. The next figure should be 4 units which, if lost, produces a line 1 1 2 3 4. Looking ahead however, another losing bet will give a line of six figures, to clear which we require three wins. If we stake a second 4 units the line will total 15 units, and this may be cleared by three bets of 5 units.

This is the beginning of a genuine reduction of capital requirement.

The effect of this method may be seen if it continues for a long time against a mild, adverse preponderance.

1 1 2 3 4 4 5 totals 20 but is an odd number of figures. The next bet is 6 units making the total 26. This, eight figures, requires to be cleared in four bets. Four bets of 7 units will do this, so we may make two such bets even should the first lose. If both lose the line becomes 1 1 2 3 4 4 5 6 7 7 totalling 40 units to be cleared in five bets.

The normal basic line for this number of losses would have been 1 1 2 3 4 5 6 7 8 9. The capital has therefore been reduced from 46 to 40, about 13%. This may not seem a lot, but if the line fails to clear for some time it will produce a comparison like this:

Normal line: 12 17 22 27 39 51 = 168
Reduced line: 5   9 13 17 22 27 =   93

The percentage has risen to 45% plus. The next stake on the normal line is 63, on the reduced line 31, less than half.

The drill is therefore to total the line at any stage—present or in advance—when it consists of an even number of figures; to divide that number of figures by two in order to discover how many bets are needed to clear the line, and then to spread the load of those bets evenly instead of making a standard increase. Thus: 10 figures require 5 bets. The total is 75, so a series of 15-unit bets may be embarked upon even should the final figure actually exceed that amount at the moment.

This will cause a certain amount of re-writing of lines at the table, but some extra clerking is the price we must pay for a diminution of capital requirement.

The Doubly Split Martingale on Single Columns

Building the system

Here is a quotation from a book on gambling. We need not take every word to be Gospel truth, for, as we have already seen in the section on the 'Immutable Law' books on gambling sometimes lay down procedures which are the result of insufficient analysis.

'It is impossible to construct a system to beat the bank at Roulette. Many players win because the odds against them are extremely small, and a streak of luck favours them. Yet, be they regular players, it is inevitable that in the long run they lose. The capital available to the bank is such that only a millionaire can confidently compete against it on equal terms and—just to ensure that none does—the House establishes a limit to the stake permitted. Over a period therefore every player must lose. Success at Roulette is only possible for short periods, when a streak of luck enables the player to flourish temporarily.'

That sounds quite authoritative. But is it? Even if it is, is there perhaps a loophole? It states that success is only possible for short periods, and with this we are inclined to give a qualified agreement. But it goes on:'—when a streak of luck enables the player to flourish—' That seems to be slightly didactic. Are there then no 'short periods' when success is to be obtained without a streak of luck? Let us see.

Agreeing (partially at least) with the mention of 'short periods', we examine what can be done in them. This does not mean that the intention is to play for ten minutes per day. Play may continue for any length of time desired. The 'short periods' we intend to suggest are simply blocks of numbers, considered in isolation from their predecessors and successors, and a system which limits itself to one particular block, abides by the result, and then turns to a fresh block. What we need to discover is blocks of numbers where a method may be immune to serious misfortune but have a really excellent chance of winning.

The 'short periods' we select are columns of 37 spins. If the column is suitable, we play; if not, we don't. We play therefore in every column which proves suitable, and may quite well be playing in about two columns out of three, i.e. two-thirds of the time, every day, all day. Any free time may be filled with a different method.

An examination of records shows that the number of times an even chance position wins in one column is an average of 18 and rarely less than 13. There are of course wild exceptions, where, for example, in 37 spins Black may win 30 times, Red only 5 and Zero twice. These are columns in which the system shown here will have to be content to suffer.

Method

The average for an even chance is 18 wins per column of 37 spins. The system bases itself on an expectation of only 12. It therefore requires a staking-plan to cope with a proportion of twelve wins against 25 losses.

Hypothetical bets are clearly necessary and the required lead of six will automatically provide them. Thus if any even chance position wins eight out of the first ten spins, the necessary hypothetical bets are there.

The lead must be six, and should be established within the first half of the column.

The opposite position is now backed with a pre-set staking-plan. This staking-plan is of extreme importance here because it must be strong enough to keep any accepted loss to a reasonable minimum but also not so strong as to demand an over high capital.

A fair example of a semi-abbreviated Split Martingale series of two lines is: 1 1 2 5 5 7 followed by 2 2 5 8 11. We play these lines against a column.

Example from play

(N)	(R)	
B	R	
	30	When No. 15 wins, Odd shows a lead of six over Even.

[Continued Overleaf

Continued from previous page]

(N) B	(R) R	
17		We therefore back Even.
	3	
	32	
	9	Staking-line 1 1 3 5 5 7
	19	
	23	
17		
35		
15		
13		Lose 1
	0	Imprisoned
28		Liberated
10		Line cleared
	7	Lose 1
	14	Cleared
10		Win 1 +1
	21	Lose 1
	3	„ 1
	1	„ 3
28		Win 5. Line cleared.
	14	Win 1 +1
	5	Lose 1
	7	Lose 1
4		Win 3. 1 unit profit. +1
	32	Win 1 +1
	7	Lose 1
15		Lose 1 Line is 1 1
	1	„ „ 1 1 3
	23	Lose 5 „ „ 1 1 3 5
10		Win 5 „ „ 1 1 3
2		Win 5. Line clear.
	19	Lose 1
28		Win 1. Line clear.
29		Lose 1
33		Lose 1
8		Win 3. 1 unit profit. +1

Total: +5 units.

Limit of profit

With a lead of six and an expectation of parity in the average column,
the opposite position requires a gain of six units in order to establish
parity. Having won 6 units therefore a check should be made to

ensure that a reasonable lead for the opposite position is still extant. To bet against a lead of six, win six and continue to back the same position when it may actually have achieved parity, wiping out the initial lead altogether, is to continue betting on a pure guess.

Different staking-plans

Any staking-plan which conforms to the wishes of the player may be used. A split doubling-up series is quite fair but the doubling-up should be confined to the first line in the series unless capital is plentiful. Perhaps 1 2 4 followed by 2 3 6 and then 3 5 9 or 3 4 8.

The Reduced Line

Recommended is the Reduced Martingale Line which we have recently constructed, p. 146.

We play a column (from play) using each of these methods. The column contains incipient disaster and so will enforce a loss except against a Complete Martingale line of 1 2 4 8 16. A player is not recommended to use such a line simply because it suits this particular column. He will encounter a couple of losses for such a line—maybe in his next column.

Meticulous hard grafting

Playing this type of column we are using a Split Martingale, trying to clear two losses by each win. The hard grafter, in his most determined mood, will undertake no bet which makes the possibility of failure greater than it should be technically. This means that if he is to win one out of three bets, the remaining number of bets in the column must not permit the ingress of extra possible failures. Put in arithmetical terms—six hypothetical bets are taken, a lead of six allowed to the non-backed position. This will leave 27 bets, say, of which 9 must be winners.

Having won the very first bet, the remaining situation is that 26 bets remain in which we have allowance for only eight winners. This breaks the 1–2 proportion which is technically necessary; should we win one out of three precisely, there will still be two bets outstanding, and these may ruin our line.

The hard grafter therefore will obstinately refuse to make another bet until the ratio has righted itself, which will occur if the non-backed position now wins twice, reducing the proportion to the correct terms—24 bets remaining to the column, eight winners permitted to cancel the losers.

This, of course, will reduce actual play to a minimum and often cut it short almost at birth. If the first bet is won, and the second would have been won had we backed it, the column might as well be abandoned, only being resuscitated if a sudden rush on the non-backed position rectifies the 1–2 ratio.

The overall situation is extremely favourable, which is why the system is recommended, but the requirement of ratio highlights the necessity for the serious player to have half-a-dozen systems at his fingertips.

(N)	(R)	
B	R	Using lines: 1 2 4, 2 3 6, 3 4 8, 4 5 10, this column,
6		starting to back Red at Spin No. 11, shows a loss of
10		24 units.
	30	Using the previous 1 1 3 5 5 7, and 2 2 4 8 11 lines
	21	it shows a loss of 22 units.
22		Using the Reduced Martingale line it shows a loss of
17		19 units.
13		Using a Complete Martingale it shows a profit of 9 units.
8		This however is bad; it is not within our province to show
29		a profit on such adverse lines, where the deviation in
2		favour of the 'wrong' position is more than 100%, i.e.
	5	25 to 12. To use a line so strong is to court disaster, not
15		especially when the deviation is even more adverse but
	12	when there is no deviation at all, and a really long run
	32	arrives both for and against us.
26		This type of loss may be considered acceptable. If it seems
28		too high, some careful manipulation of the Reduced
2		Martingale line can improve it.
13		
	1	
13		
29		
31		
35		
	18	
6		
	36	
17		
33		
	27	

(N)	(R)
B	R
8	
	7
22	
20	
11	
	14
	19
24	

Drill for reducing the Reduced Martingale Line

The reduced Split Martingale we have constructed will provide many comfortable wins. The hard grafter will therefore rely upon these for his profit while elsewhere concentrating upon his main task—not to lose.

This he does by the acceptance of loss, by writing off, and by the refusal to permit his stake to rise too quickly. The line is therefore kept low by recommencement unless it contains sufficient loss to demand an initial higher stake. Thus:

Playing the same column we start off with two wins, arriving when No. 5 and 32 win. The line then goes 1 1 2 3 when a win of 4 units reduces it to 1 2. The hard grafter accepts this, puts it aside and recommences his line from the beginning.

Now come four losers and one winner for which he will use precisely the same drill, 1 1 2 3 reduced to 1 2 and this residue set aside, the line restarted.

The next seven spins, Nos. 6, 36, 17, 33, 27, 8 and 7 produce nothing. At this point the hard grafter gets the impression that the deviation is moving, if not towards him, at least not so strongly away from him, and considers that a mite of optimism may perhaps be permitted; but still a very small mite until something more definite emerges in his favour.

The next three spins produce 1 1 2 and the fourth gives a win of 3 units to reduce this to 1. The hard grafter decides not to set this 1 unit aside but to keep it in the line. The gambler, seeing this, would have something ironical to say about such 'boldness', but it would have no effect. The hard grafter takes 1 unit from those set aside to make the line 1 1 and leave his loss residue at 5 units instead of 6 units. He stakes 2 units now but loses, shakes his head at such excessive optimism and concedes a loss on the entire line of 9 units minus the original 2 units won, a final total of 7 units lost.

Obviously his method will consistently reduce his profits, but not in those columns which give him a favourable preponderance. For example, had he backed Black instead of Red in this same column, starting at Spin No. 11 where No. 5 wins, he would have won 9 units. Even a Complete Martingale which risks the loss of an entire capital, would have won only 17 units.

We may note that this loss of 7 units is actually what would have been achieved by the use of a completely flat, unvarying stake of 1 unit, a method which makes no effort to improve upon what the wheel offers and, theoretically at least, takes no risk whatever. This is against an adverse deviation of 100%.

We return to our gaming 'authority'. 'It is impossible to construct a system to beat the bank—.' We wonder! 'Many players win because the odds—are extremely small and a streak of luck favours them.' The odds certainly are small, but what about the streak of luck? What streak of luck favoured us here? A streak of bad luck—yes, indeed, encountering such a deviation. And while we may not have 'flourished' nobody can say that we have been annihilated. '—only a millionaire can compete—' That does not seem to apply. Playing in half-crown units we could have tackled this column with a total capital of thirty-five shillings, and still have half of it left.

The conclusion we must inevitably draw is that writers who state that Roulette is a game of blind chance are being over-confident.

This brick wall approach to the problem of Roulette will not appeal to the adventurous, smacking too much of the Maginot mind. 'This line is impregnable.' All very well—until someone went round. Yet the Maginot approach of extreme caution must be adopted if we are to win consistently while, concurrently, we must prepare alternative defences for when the 'enemy' attempts to 'go round'. This brings us to the method which bets against the repetition of a previous achievement.

We take the easiest method to be read on the card—Black and Red.

Drill

Note what the colour achieved at its last essay. Bet first that it will not equal this. If it does, bet that it will surpass it. If this also loses, retire until the colour changes and do similarly against the other colour.

This is a recommended method. Its disadvantage is that it is out of action for a considerable time, especially when long runs of wins for a position are prevalent. This may be largely overcome by backing more than one position, using, say, High and Low also as targets. More than this is of course possible, but will require meticulous book-keeping.

We play a column, using a Reduced Split Martingale Line

1   1   2   3   4   4   5   6   7   7 etc.

The first five spins are ignored as we do not know whether the first win by No. 16 is in isolation or at the end of a run. No. 26 wins at Spin 6.

(N)	(R)	
B	R	
	16	No. 26 wins. Black's previous achievement was a double-
22		ton. Bet that this will not be equalled. 1 unit on Red.
10		Loses. Line is 1. Bet again that the previous doubleton
	30	will not be equalled. 1 unit Black. Wins. Line clear.
	3	Wait for the change to Red, which also produced a
26		doubleton last time.
13		
8		
	7	No. 7 wins. Stake 1 unit on Black. Wins. Line +.
24		No. 24 wins but offers no bet. We will bet on Red if the
	19	next win produces a doubleton by Black, but it does not.
	3	No. 19 wins. Red having previously produced a singleton
33		we bet that this will not be another. 1 unit Red. Wins.
11		Line + +
	34	
35		Wait for the change, ready to bet that Black will not
0		produce another singleton. No. 33 wins. 1 unit on Black.
28		Wins. Line + + +
	30	
24		Wait for the change. No. 34 wins. We bet against a
22		doubleton. 1 unit Black. Wins. Line + + + +
	5	No. 35 wins. 1 unit Red. Loses. 1 unit Black. Lost when
31		No. 30 wins. Line + + + + 1 1
	18	
2		
13		Bet against a Red singleton now. 2 unit. Loses. Line
	9	+ + + + 1 1 2
	18	No. 24 wins. Bet against a Black doubleton. 3 units Red.
	32	Loses. Line + + + + 1 1 2 3. 4 units Black. Loses.

[Continued Overleaf

Continued from previous page]

(N)	(R)	
B	R	
	27	Line + + + + 1 1 2 3 4
11		
	5	No. 5 wins. Bet against a singleton. Loses when No. 31
	32	wins. Line + + + + 1 1 2 3 4 4. Bet against a Black
	16	doubleton, 5 units Red. Wins. Line + + + + 1 2 3 4
29		

No. 18 wins. Bet against a Red singleton, 4 units Black. Loses.
Line + + + + 1 2 3 4 4.

No. 2 wins. Bet against a Black singleton. 5 units Black. Wins.
Line + + + + 2 3 4.

Wait for the change. Bet against a Red singleton when No. 9 wins.
4 units Red. Wins. Line + + + + 2 3

Wait for the change. No. 11 wins. Bet against Black doubleton.
4 units Red. Wins. Line + + + + 1.

Wait. When No. 16 wins bet that Red will not produce a four-timer.
2 units Black. Wins. Line + + + + +.

Following the Dominant

Every croupier will advise that it is important to 'follow the wheel' and not to bet against it. This is all very well but in practice it makes no difference whether we do one or the other. The wheel has no bias. Nevertheless it is true that the relentless insistence of a particular position winning when we are betting against it is more apparent mentally than is the reversal of the immediate trend, so there may be some psychological advantage in playing with the wheel. There are many systems based upon this and we take the extreme, using the six basic even chance positions only.

Drill

Stake 1 unit on each position produced by the winning spin. Use a staking-plan 1 2 4 plus 2 4 8 and carry each position right through without hedging, a practice which will be clarified on examination of the example.

(N) B	(R) R	Stake			BR				OE (Lines)			HL		
	25	R1	O1	H1										
22		B2	E2	H1	1				1			+		
	7	R4	O4	L2	1	2			1	2		1		
24		B2	E2	H4	1	2	4		1	2	4	1	2	
10		B2	E2	L2	1	4			1	4		1	2	4
6		B2	E2	L4	1	2			1	2		1	4	
	36	R4	E2	H4	1	2	2		1			1	4	2
28		B8	E1	H2	1	2	2	4	+			1	4	
24		B2	E2	H2	1				+			1	2	
22		B1	E1	H2	+				+			1		
	12	R2	E1	L4	1				+			1	2	
15		B4	O2	L1	1	2			1			+		
	16	R2	E4	L1	1	2	4		1	2		+		
	14	R2	E1	L1	1	4			+			+		
20		B4	E1	H2	1	4	2		+			1		

[Continued Overleaf

Continued from previous page]

(N) B	(R) R	Stake	BR	Lines OE	HL
	9	R8 O2 L4	1 4 2 4	1	1 2
	7	R2 O1 L1	1	+	+
15		B4 O1 L1	1 2	+	+
	5	R2 O1 L1	1 2 4	+	+
	25	R2 O1 H2	1 4	+	1
10		R2 O1 H4	1 2	+	1 2
13		B4 E2 L2	1 2 2	1	1 2 4
			1	1 2	1 4

The first number is noted and a stake of 1 unit placed on each of its positions. High wins, the others lose. High remains at 1 unit, the others demand 2 units.

When the initial Martingale line 1 2 4 has failed, instead of rushing to 6 units and risking an eventual really bad Martingale disaster we use a second line of 2 4 8, returning to 2 units each time a win is made.

The result here is +19 units with 9 units outstanding.

This type of line, a treble, is most informative. One column or even this half-column would sway the experienced player to switch from the dominant colour to the non-dominant. Black–Red has broken even this way, using a double Martingale line. It must inevitably be a winner if the trend continues and the non-dominant is backed. Dominant Odd–Even is doing very well. High–Low is debatable, and might well be abandoned on the table for a while, still keeping the score however in order to note which way the deviation eventually goes. At present the position clearly cannot make up its mind whether to play dominant or non-dominant. When it does we will start staking on it. Alternatively we could play an Alembert on High or on Low, the pattern being clearly favourable.

Note: The above layout cannot be too easy to read at the first attempt. The best routine is to note the number which has last won, then to check the stakes which must be placed upon the next spin according to the respective lines extant, then to see what number does win the next spin, and finally amend the line accordingly. Back then to the number which has won to decide the stakes to be next placed.

The mention of 'hedging' perhaps requires some explanation still. It is clarified in the very first coup. We stake 1 unit each on Red High and Odd. We win on High but lose on the others. Without hedging this goes down on the lines as plus 1 for High, minus 1 for the others. Hedging would amalgamate the results as minus 1, and decide where to put it. Backing the dominant, the dominant on High being up to now successful, we may decide to leave the other lines clear and put the 1 unit loss in the HL line.

It is really early days to make such decisions, because no concrete evidence is available, so the thing becomes a pure guess. So we make it. But later on, some ingenious shuffling between lines might well be undertaken, the line doing badly swapping stakes with the line which appears to be doing well. On the principle of reinforcing success this method has much to recommend it.

Experience will be necessary lest the player get tied into knots with his accounting, which is why so much is provided for the inexperienced player to use as settling-in material. It would not be seriously out of order to suggest that some mild time-and-motion study of his physical movements at the table might be of benefit. Also it is better for the inexperienced player either to play at a French table—knowing the language or not is immaterial; if he wins he will be paid and if he loses his money will just disappear—here the game is slower, or, should he insist upon an American table, deliberately to play only alternate spins. And, of course, record only alternate spins. This will not affect any system except Les Voisins, which will not yet be in his orbit. The results at the table form a pattern but within that pattern is a perfectly good second pattern for alternate spins, or any other fraction of total spins, or any permutation of selected spins. Every sequence of numbers must eventually form some sort of pattern.

Variation of Staking-plan

Economy is achieved by using a gradually rising flat stake as a staking-plan. The stake is 1 unit and is increased to 2 units only when the line reaches eight losers. This is a good system and takes advantage of every run in every position. It does however cause some frustration from time to time, a line running to six or seven single losers, returning to nil and then increasing again to six or seven.

We play a column which includes this feature so that the drawbacks of the method may be appreciated as are the advantages.

The length of line before increase is at the discretion of the player.

A precaution against the adverse run and corresponding rise of stake is to limit the decrease of the initial line when it is in process of being cleared by a higher stake, e.g. the line reads 1 1 1 1 1 1 1 1 and a stake of 2 units is played. A few wins and losses give an advantage of two wins, thus decreasing the line to 1 1 1 1. Reversion should now be made to 1 unit.

This type of limitation of decrease is subject to judgment according to the time-factor in conjunction with the number of write-offs. We know that with the Zero effect being always adverse we should write off at least one spin by superior staking per column, and preferably more. Thus should the line go up and down for some time the attempt should be made to write off a number of losses to correspond with and compensate for the columns actually played.

(N) B	(R) R	Targets			Stake on each	Line						
6		B	L	E	1							
	19	R	H	O	1	1	1	1				
4		B	L	E	1	1	1	1	1	1	1 (A 'good' start!)	
15		B	L	O	1	1	1	1	1	1		
	9	R	L	O	1	1	1	1	1			
	30	R	H	E	1	1	1	1	1	1		
26		B	H	E	1	1	1	1	1			
28		B	H	E	1	1						
33		B	H	O	1	–						
6		B	L	E	1	1						
	16	R	L	E	1	–						
22		B	H	E	1	1						
	3	R	L	O	1	1	1	1	1			
35		B	H	O	1	1	1	1	1	1		
	32	R	H	E	1	1	1	1	1	1	1	
	18	R	L	E	1	1	1	1	1	1		
28		B	H	E	1	1	1	1	1	1	1	
26		B	H	E	1	1	1	1				
8		B	L	E	1	1	1					
	27	R	H	O	1	1	1	1	1	1		
28		B	H	E	1	1	1	1	1	1	1	
6		B	L	E	1	1	1	1	1	1		
10		B	L	E	1	1	1					
22		B	H	E	1	1						
	32	R	H	E	1	–						
	14	R	L	E	1	+						
	34	R	H	E	1	++						
	12	R	L	E	1	+++						
	5	R	L	O	1	++++						

(N)	(R)	Targets	Stake on each	Line
B	**R**			
11		B L O	1	+ + + + +
	12	R L E	1	+ + + +
	34	R H E	1	+ + + + +
	36	R H E	1	+ + + + + + + +
15		B L O	1	1 1 1
20		B H E	1	1 1 1 1
26		B H E	1	1
	27	R H O	1	1 1
	7	R L O	1	1
10		B L E	1	1 1
	22		1	1 1 1

Result: 8 units won, line outstanding 3 units.

Switch to this method is inviting when there appear to be runs of reasonable length as opposed to quick alternations.

Comment: An excellent secondary system, suitable for the experienced player in suitable circumstances, especially suitable for a second stage method when the beginner needs something more advanced than his initial methods.

More Dominants

On the principle that the dominant should be followed, thus avoiding the frustration characteristic of the player betting continuously against a long run, various methods have been devised, and, of course, scores more may be.

Following three

Await a run of three for any of the six even chance positions (standard) or any of the three even chance alternations, i.e.

	B RRR	or	R BBB
	O EEE		E OOO
	H LLL		L HHH

BB	R B R	or	RR	B R B
HH	L H L		LL	H L H
OO	E O E		EE	O E O

Bet for the series to continue.

Thus with B RRR back Red. Should it win, stop. Should it lose,
stop. Wait for the next sequence. Any sequence will do. We bet 1 unit
on a continuation of Red after B RRR and lose. Now comes BB R
B R. Bet 2 units on the continuation of the alternation, i.e. B. It loses.
Next series comes E OOO Back Odd according to the staking-plan
being used. Thus, using a Simple Alembert the next bet will be
3 units. Using a Contra Alembert it will remain—as would have been
the second bet also—1 unit. Using a (Contra) Flexible Alembert,
start 5 units, the first three bets would be 5 units, 4 units, 3 units.
Using a straight Martingale, the three bets would be 1 2 4. Straight
Martingale with an insurance bet at No. 2 would produce a line
1 1 3; the insurance bet at No. 3 would produce 1 2 3,
Only one bet in this variation is made for each series, win or lose.

The Complete Dominant

Back the first colour to win. If it does so, repeat the bet and continue
with 1 unit until it changes. Change with it, using the selected
staking-plan, 2 units normally, 1 unit if an insurance bet is set for
No. 2, 1 unit if Contra Alembert is used.
Continue to back the fresh colour until it loses, when a change is
made to the new dominant, each change of course producing a
differentiation of stake according to the plan in use.

All three

The same method, guaranteeing that the player will be 'on' the whole
time in any long run of any of the standard six even chance positions,
is employed for those positions.
Good book-keeping will be necessary if all the positions are backed
simultaneously. If this is too much, back two only.

(N)	(R)	
B	R	Simple Alembert used.
	34	It is decided to back the dominant colour and the domi-
	18	nant level. B and R, H and L.
29		
	36	Stake 1 unit on Red and High when No. 34 wins the first
33		spin.

(N)	(R)						
B	R						
35							
8		Wins	BR			HL	
24		18	+			1	
	21	29	1			1	2
		36	1	2		—	written off
		33	1	2	3	+	
		35	1	2	3̸	+	
		8	1	2̸		1	
		24	1̸			1	2
		21	1			—	written off

BR has won 4 units, with 1 in outstanding line.
HL has won 2 units.

OE would have produced a line: + 12̸3̸3 winning 3 units but leaving
a line of 6 units outstanding.

Changing with the Wheel

This method endeavours not only to be 'on' any long run of dominants but also on any long run of non-dominants. Losing series come
when the table changes quickly from one to the other, apparently
following the player—adversely. Back the dominant.
After three consecutive losses, change to the non-dominant. After
three consecutive losses on the non-dominant, change back. Continue in the same manner, changing with the fluctuations of the wheel.

(N)	(R)	Martingale 1 2 4; 2 4 8; 3 5 10 staking-plan.
B	R	Backing the changing colour.
28		Line
10		+
	19	1
34		1 2
19		+
10		+
33		+
	14	1
22		1 2
	9	1 2 4 Change to non-dominant. Use 2 4 8.
	1	1 2 4 2
11		1 2 2
17		1 2 2 2

[Continued Overleaf

Continued from previous page]

(N) B	(R) R					
	23	1	2			
2		1	Return to 1 2 4			
8		1	2			
29		1	2	4	Change to dominant. Use 2 4 8	
15		1	2	2		
2		1	2			
28		1	Return to 1 2 4			
	16	1	2			
	36	+				
	1	+				
4		1				
13		+				
	7	1				
22		1	2			
	34	1	2	4	Change to non-dominant. Use 2 4 8	
17		1	2	2		
	12	1	2			
20		1	Return to 1 2 4			
8		1	2			
35		1	2	4	Change to dominant. Use 2 4 8	
26		1	2	2		
	3	1	2	2	2	
11		1	2	2	2	4
31		1	2			

Result of column: + 7 units with line outstanding of 12.

Note: At Spin No. 15, No. 2 winning, a return to the basic stake-line 1 2 4 is directed. Here the player has made a technical error, using a bet of 2 units which is the first bet in his 2 4 8 line, not his 1 2 4 line. He is therefore attempting to clear a win in two bets, i.e. 2 4 instead of in three bets 1 2 4. He does the same thing five spins later and again at Spin No. 32. This may in adverse circumstances have a deleterious effect upon his sequence, either on capital or cancellation. He is, in arithmetical terms, using 6 units in two bets instead of 7 units in three; six-sevenths of his immediate ammunition in two-thirds of the allotted time. He is also reducing his chances of winning each particular bet from 7–1 in his favour (progression of three bets) to 3–1 in his favour (progression of two bets), the alternative being to continue with his 2 4 8 line unnecessarily.

Bread & Butter Split Martingale: Graduated Progressions

This is an extension of the little man's system we saw earlier. There are extensions and variations, and most of them are good. This type of play may be *recommended*.

Drill

Use four hypothetical bets. Staking-plan straight Martingale 1 2 4. Follow all even chance positions.

Already this has much in its favour; the series 1 2 4 has an expectation of loss only once in eight commencements. (Roulette odds being (bar the Zero) always perfect, this should be taken for granted. If a play wins 7 units for a 1 unit stake the odds will be a natural 7–1 against its success. If it loses 7 units against a 1 unit profit the odds will naturally be 7–1 in favour of success.)

Once the line has been lost a fresh line with an increased profit for success is used to wipe out the original lost line. This may be adjusted according to capital, but it is important that the available capital be *used*.

      1st line: 1 2 4. 2nd line: 2 4 8 is best.
                          3rd line: 3 6 12 is best.
                          4th line: 4 8 16 is best.

To the small player however these subsequent lines seem dangerous. It is open to him then to use lines as:

      2nd line: 1 2 4 (a repeat)
                  2 2 4 (2 insurance bets)
                  2 3 5 (1 insurance bet)
                  2 3 6 (reduced profit)
                  2 4 6 (1 insurance bet)

All these are aimed at an avoidance of increase capital. They are none of them ideal and should normally only come into play when there is a genuine danger of the entire capital being lost. Yet, in such circumstances, it is probably a better play not to increase the stake after the loss of 1 2 4 but to *decrease* it; to play a completely flat stake of 1 unit to get the 'feel of the table' before making any increase. The point to remember is the one made first: that a 1 2 4 line has a 7-1 chance of success, and therefore so has a 2 4 8 line. A 2 4 8 line will wipe out a lost 1 2 4 line (reduce it to 1) in three coups. But decrease it to, for example, 2 3 6 and it will require three *immediate* coups to produce a similar result. Each immediate coup being even money it must take at least twice as long to clear the line with 2 3 6 than it does with 2 4 8, and during this period the danger is ever present that the secondary line will also be lost.

The gambler, faced with a 1 2 4 line lost will—if he is a good gambler—endeavour to erase it at a blow with a second line 7 14 28. He is 7-1-on to succeed. Can he be faulted? Technically, no. For that play we have no quarrel, only, in fact, admiration. The one proviso is that the player should not only be able to afford it but be able to attack once more if it is lost. Once in eight times he will meet not a loss of 7 units but of 56 units. If he can confidently face that and get down to serious clearance of it—all right; if not, the gambler's play carries too great a threat to be used by the hard grafter.

Further targets for the Bread and Butter Doubly Split Martingale

Following the Dominant

This attempts to be on every long run, so therefore should be used when the table seems to be producing long runs. Swift alternations simply mean frustration through inability to play for most of the time and non-success when play is possible.

Drill

Use the standard six even chances and also the three alternations. Wait until one position has repeated itself twice, producing a run of three. Stake 1 unit on that position. If it wins repeat the bet and continue to do so until it loses. The moment it loses, cease playing and look for another target.

The Lengthening Line

A loss here will produce a line of 1. The next target faces this loss and the line used must take it into account. The same 1 2 4 line may be used, turning the initial bet into an insurance bet. If profit is desired the first bet must be 2 units, but it is not advisable—unless capital is large—to use a 2 4 8 line at once, while to use simply 2 4 is to reduce the chances of success. Therefore an insurance bet should be introduced, perhaps with a line 2 3 5 or, using a four-figure line—2 3 5 10 or an interior Split Martingale—2 3 5 8.

On balance the initial insurance bet of 1 unit is the most practicable—the normal 1 2 4 line repeated.

This system enables the player to win on every coup for every even chance position which extends for more than three. As there are plenty of coups of ten or more it can prove very satisfying.

Following the Change

A recommended method. It consists of waiting until one of the even chance positions produces a doubleton and is then succeeded by a change. To defeat the method the position must produce a doubleton or more, then a change to the opposite position for precisely one coup, returning to the previous position for at least three coups. (Or more, if the staking-plan covers more.)

Thus, should we use a simple 1 2 4 line, and follow this with a secondary line, we lose to, for example,

$$-BB \ R \ BBB \quad \text{or} \quad -OO \ E \ OOO \text{ etc.}$$

Should our line be 1 2 4 8 an extra coup for the continuation is required to defeat us. Players who follow the wheel will appreciate that this type of completely isolated win for a position is basically against the nature of their philosophy.

Combination

Building up our own method we may use this system which follows the wheel in conjunction with a simple hypothetical bet method which goes against the wheel.

Thus: we discover four hypothetical coups and stake against the continuation. We win at some stage in our line, and by doing so produce the change which is required above, thereby being automatically presented with a fresh target. The first win was against the wheel; we are now betting with the wheel. A comparison of the progress of the two methods may now enable us to concentrate upon one to the exclusion of the other, one having done well, the other badly. It also enables us, should one be threatening trouble, to insure heavily on that line while increasing the stake on the line which is doing well.

We play 'Following the Change' against the last of our 'Practice columns':

(N)	(R)	
	32	The last column is selected simply because the author's
11		MSS is so bound that the last column (near the edge) is
15		easier to read that the first, (nearer the margin).
20		Spin four gives two targets: High and Even. Take both.
33		High wins. Even wins at the third bet. (Playing all-out.
	7	Details of alternative method will be found at the end.)
	34	
	7	
4		Playing all-out a target of Low arrives concurrently with
26		the second bet on Even. It wins on the second bet.
	3	(Now +3)
0		No. 26 gives a target of High which causes a line–loss.
8		Concurrently, No. 3 has given a target of Odd which
6		reduces the line to 2 4. Use 2 4 8 as second line. No. 15
15		gives target of Odd. Wins. Line is 4. In passing we
	16	missed—as we are always likely to do at the table if not
8		careful—another Bet produced by No. 3, i.e. Red, and
	9	this caused a second loss of a first line, so our line should
	21	now be 1 2 4 4.
	18	
20		No. 9 gives Odd. Line 1 4 4
31		No. 21 gives High. Line 1 2 4
	18	No. 18 gives Even. Line 1 4
	1	No. 31 gives Odd. Line 1 2
	14	No. 18 gives Low. Line 1
17		No. 18 also gives Red. Line cleared with 1 unit plus.
	18	
	5	
13		

(N)	(R)	
	14	No. 13 gives Black. No. 14 gives Even.
	1	Both win, Even somewhat delayed by an intrusive
11		Zero.
0		
	12	In the meantime No. 11 has given Black. This wins with
	36	No. 2, which immediately gives Black, winning imme-
2		diately. No. 36 has given High, but the result is not
10		known.

Result: +8 units.

This is a good column, appreciated by the hard grafter. 8 units in twenty minutes is 24 units an hour, 72 units in a three hour session. Good wages.

Hedging

Playing all-out we backed two positions, one of which won immediately, the other winning on the third bet.
The hard grafter, in tenacious and conscientious mood, would have won nothing. Having backed two targets and found himself winning one, losing one, he would have called it square and waited for another target.
His basic philosophy, it should be recalled, is *not to lose*. Breaking even he has not lost; he is therefore satisfied.

Variation

Having broken even on these bets and feeling slightly adventurous, he may recommence his series on the lost bet position. This turns the win on the first bet into an insurance bet for his second position line. His second bet is therefore still 1 unit with the chance of success increased in that it now takes four losses to beat him instead of three.

Les Voisins

The lure of this method is that with one success per full column it can turn the $2\cdot7\%$ advantage for the bank into about a 16% advantage for the punter.

The method differs from the ordinary type of system in that it is based not upon the manipulation of arithmetic but upon human fallibility. There is sound sense in this. The wheel is totally unreceptive to any outside influence, but the croupier, who is the only intrusion of humanity into the manipulations of the game, is subject to the normal failings of humanity.

It is incontrovertible as well as being perfectly natural that any person performing a set routine tends to fall into a set rhythm. The croupier, working at the wheel for hours every day, his attention mainly concentrated upon the placing of bets and the payment of winnings—all of which require absolute precision, whereas the turn of the wheel and the spin of the ball do not—inevitably falls into such a rhythm for a good part of the time. The theory supposes therefore that each individual croupier will during a certain period tend to favour certain sections of the wheel.

With set speed and unvarying force this must be true, even though absolute consistency may never be attained in two consecutive spins.

Croupier drill

The croupier turns the wheel clockwise and anti-clockwise alternately, spins the ball against the turn and delivers it from a point immediately above the last winning number.

Note: this is correct drill, but in some casinos it is not adhered to strictly. If not, the method Les Voisins loses its *raison d'être*, so should not be employed.

If the ball is delivered from an unknown position, similar turn and spin will produce similar spin-distance but something quite different for number-section.

Drill

Having checked that the croupier delivers the ball correctly, a note of the first two winning numbers should be taken. The relation between them is noted and the play deduced from this; but reserved for the second spin away because Les Voisins is used on *alternate*, not consecutive spins.

We assume, for purposes of illustration, that the first two winning numbers are 26 and 10. These are almost directly opposite each other. Thus the croupier's use of wheel-turn and finger-spin combined has caused the ball to move around the wheel a number of revolutions plus one-half of a revolution.

A further spin is observed and the relation between it and the second spin is noted. Now, working from that last number the play is made according to the first observation, while the next play will be made according to the second observation.

This is because the mobility of the croupier's hand is a genuine factor. When the wheel turns one way his hand goes to the front, palm forward; when it turns the other way his hand goes to the rear, palm away from the table. In this second position the fingers have slightly more play, just as in lawn-tennis the backhand has a greater length of swing than has the forehand.

Collection of Data

Note the way the ball was travelling, clockwise or anti-clockwise. Note the winning number.

It is necessary to know which way the ball travels in order to estimate whether to back a number short of a complete revolution or in excess of a complete revolution. The number of revolutions is of no import.

This data is best determined by an examination of the wheel card, considering the wheel to be stationary, the ball alone to move. (The cashier or croupier will provide a card.)

Drill

The first winning number is No. 26. No data available except that the ball travelled anti-clockwise.

The second winning number is No. 10. The ball going clockwise produced an opposite.

The third winning number was No. 22. The ball going anti-clockwise produced a number ten short of a full revolution.

Bets are now placed according to the data collated between Nos. 26 and 10, i.e. an opposite *et ses deux voisins*, its two neighbours either side, Nos. 25, 17, 34, 6, 27.

The ball, going clockwise to No. 4, falls short of the pivot number 34 by five spaces. Data for the alternate next spin is corrected according.

Data from Spin No. 3 is now used at Spin No. 5. Ten numbers short of the winning No. 4, ball going anti-clockwise, gives No. 7, plus two neighbours: 18, 29, 7, 28, 12.

No. 29 wins. Ball has under-run by one space only. Data is corrected accordingly.

Notation

Simple and clear notation makes this initially slightly complicated method simple.

Clock.	Anti.
opp.	−10
opp−5	−9

No more is needed. All the necessary information is included and the corrections to data are precise and easy to read. The notation is read:

opp. = when the ball is travelling clockwise, back the number opposite to that which last won.

−10 = when the ball is travelling anti-clockwise, back the number ten short of a full revolution.

opp−5 = when the ball is travelling clockwise back the number five short of the number directly opposite the one which last won.

−9 = when the ball is travelling anti-clockwise, back the number nine short of the number which last won.

The attraction of the method does not lie in its infallibility because it is no more infallible than is any other system, but in the fact that whatever advantage may derive from it costs nothing. If we bet at random we still have five chances in 37 to win. If we bet according to previous data we have the same chances, but if it so happens that our data was correct the bet is no longer random, so our chances are enormously improved.

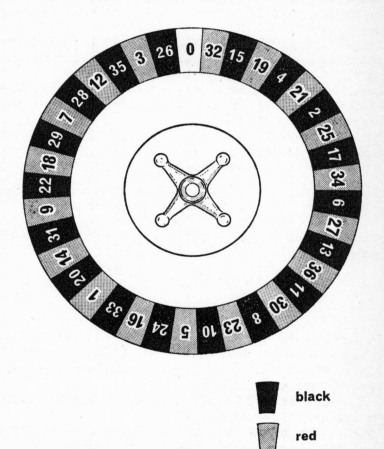

black

red

0   no colour

Table of Voisins

As the croupier, especially at an American table, may not be able to place every bet, it is convenient to have this Table of Neighbours handy.

12	35	3	26	0	32	15	19	4
5	24	16	33	1	20	14	31	9
15	19	4	21	2	25	17	34	6
7	28	12	35	3	26	0	32	15
0	32	15	19	4	21	2	25	17
30	8	23	10	5	24	16	33	1
2	25	17	34	6	27	13	36	11
9	22	18	29	7	28	12	35	3
13	36	11	30	8	23	10	5	24
1	20	14	31	9	22	18	29	7
11	30	8	23	10	5	24	16	33
6	27	13	36	11	30	8	23	10
18	29	7	28	12	35	3	26	0
17	34	6	27	13	36	11	30	8
16	33	1	20	14	31	9	22	18
3	26	0	32	15	19	4	21	2
23	10	5	24	16	33	1	20	14
4	21	2	25	17	34	6	27	13
14	31	9	22	18	29	7	28	12
26	0	32	15	19	4	21	2	25
24	16	33	1	20	14	31	9	22
32	15	19	4	21	2	25	17	34
20	14	31	9	22	18	29	7	28
36	11	30	8	23	10	5	24	16
8	23	10	5	24	16	33	1	20
19	4	21	2	25	17	34	6	27
28	12	35	3	26	0	32	15	19
25	17	34	6	27	13	36	11	30
22	18	29	7	28	12	35	3	26
31	9	22	18	29	7	28	12	35
27	13	36	11	30	8	23	10	5
33	1	20	14	31	9	22	18	29
35	3	26	0	32	15	19	4	21
10	5	24	16	33	1	20	14	31
21	2	25	17	34	6	27	13	36
29	7	28	12	35	3	26	0	32
34	6	27	13	36	11	30	8	23

The Long Haul

An interesting system which can prove very profitable if handled with care but which may require a large capital. It is played on any of the even chances, or, should sufficient capital be available, on three simultaneously. Partners may even play all six even chances simultaneously, each taking three. The requirement for success is to win 50% of bets, which, disregarding the Zero, is precisely what the Roulette table offers—over a period.

The initial stake is 1 unit which remains until a loss is incurred. This starts the line: 1.

The next stake is 3 units, repeated until a bet wins, when the 1 is crossed off and the stake becomes 5 units. This stake remains until each 3 has been crossed off, leaving only 5s in the line. The stake then becomes 7 units, rising by 2 units each time until the line is clear. Each figure crossed off represents a gain of 2 units. As it also represents one loss cancelled by one win, it means that 2 units have been won for each two spins of the wheel, or, alternately 1 unit for every spin, disregarding the Zero.

Here is a line in play:

$$\cancel{1} \quad \cancel{3} \quad \cancel{3} \quad \cancel{3} \quad \cancel{5} \quad \cancel{5} \quad \cancel{5} \quad \cancel{5} \quad \cancel{7} \quad \cancel{7} \quad \cancel{7} \quad 7 \quad 7$$

The stake is at present 9 units, two stakes of 7 units remaining to be cleared. The gain at present is 22 units, eleven losses having been cancelled.

Less capital

The above line genuinely requires a large capital as the line may run into the fifties or more against a bad adverse run, so to reduce this we may raise the stake only 1 unit instead of two. This naturally halves the profit, this being now 1 unit for each two spins of the wheel. Nevertheless, this accords with correct technique, because we do not set out to win the maximum but *to win*. Once we can win, more profit is obtained not by more winning bets but by increasing the unit staked.

Caution

This method basically disregards the Zero effect. Yet this is the one thing which really operates against its success. Genuine success demands that we win half the bets. On average, against the Zero effect, this simply cannot be done. Anyone who does it is simply being lucky. Therefore some safety-valve must be incorporated so that this continual adverse reaction may be offset. The obvious one is the write-off.

In the above example line, 22 units have been won while two sevens remain, 14 units outstanding. These should be written off at once. The profit is 8 units in 24 spins which is extremely good. This is therefore the time to be satisfied and to start a fresh line with a stake of 1 unit.

Writing-off may also be done by reduction of stake as well as complete elimination. Thus a line: 1 2 2 2 2 2 2 3 3 3 4 4 5 5 5 6 6 6 7 7 using the single raise, shows a profit of 16 units with 26 outstanding. Fearing that this may send the capital requirement too high, these may be reduced. The decision is to reduce the profit to half, 8 units. This may be used to reduce the outstanding bets from 6 6 7 7 to 4 4 5 5. Alternately, one bet may be eliminated, leaving 6 7 7 and the remaining 2 units be used to reduce the two final stakes, leaving 6 6 6.

The Very Long Haul

Over an extended period a player may expect to break even on an even chance position except for the adverse effect of the Zero. This has a double effect, against the chosen position and for the opposite. For example:

(N)	(R)
B	R
13	
28	
0	
	9
2	

Red wins a coup but it is merely a liberated coup which is then lost.

6

0

8

14

Black's coup is a loss to Red even though its 'liberation' fails to consolidate.

The result of this effect is to make it impossible to bet on both sides of the table without losing on both sides on average. To succeed on one side, even should an average be obtained, the effect of the Zero must be counterbalanced. This can be done in a short period by weight of money, although the occasional freak will spell disaster. But without weight of money it can only be done by the principle of writing-off.

The Very Long Haul is one which can only be undertaken by the player with extreme patience, and an ambition to win a small number of units over a long time, not expecting to do other than lose in many sessions but overall expecting to show a profitable balance.

It consists in playing one even chance—or more simultaneously if so desired—at absolutely even stakes until a consecutive run of four losers—equivalent to our standard four hypothetical bets—is encountered, and then increasing the stake sufficiently to be able to write-off two losers for one winner.

As the expectation for Zero is—on average—the loss to the player of 1 unit per column, while the expectation for adverse runs of four— see Table of Frequencies—is just over two per column, the ability to write off the Zero effect is there, and should in time—again on average—produce a gain of 1 unit per column. It is true that increasing the stake against a run of four will prove to be a losing bet half the time, but, providing it is also a winning bet half the time, and the remainder of the increased stake can be cancelled by winning half, losing half, the effect is genuinely there; the line will have been shortened by one coup (slightly over on average) per column.

Increase of Stake

As the write-off has the fundamental task of cancelling two bets by one, it follows that it must require an increase of stake to a doubled

amount. This, however, may be to an extent minimised if small bets
are still extant in the line. Thus a line 1 1 1 + + 1 1 1 1 1 (a
consecutive run of four losses) demands a stake of 2 units. Should
this become a run of eight the final, uncancelled part of the line will
show 1 1 1 1 2 2 2 2 and require a further increase of stake. Were
the line 2 2 2 2 this would have to be to 4 units. As it stands however 3 units is sufficient until the single units have been wiped off.

Don't forget!

Here we see that we 'owe' the line two write-offs. Standard procedure
with four losers in a run demands an increase of stake. We increase.
The bet wins. Two figures are cancelled by one win. That is the
required amount, so the method falls back to the parity stake
immediately.

However, in a situation where two write-off bets are 'owing' we must
supply them, and the stake may rise accordingly. 1 1 1 2 2 2 2
Bet 3 units. It wins. Line is now 1 1 2 2 2, but we still owe one
write-off so the next bet is 3 units again. If this loses we must continue with flat threes until they are cleared and another three pays
the outstanding account, or we again encounter a run of four which
increases our debt to two write-offs again. Once the two write-offs
are cleared, return is made to parity. The exception to this is when
parity clears off the final bet at that level. Thus, the line is 1 1 1 1
2 2. The bet is 2 units, the necessary write-offs previous to this have
been 'paid'. Twice we win two units, leaving 1 1 1 1. There is no
objection now to a continuation with 2 units for one bet only.

In Practice

Backing first Black and then Red right through the practice columns
1–10, page 212, we find that both colours finish winning, Black +11,
Red +5 units over the ten columns. A marked preponderance for
Black in the early columns is gradually counteracted by a gentle
swing to Red which finishes better. This appears to jell accurately
with the theoretical 1 unit per column we expected.
Nevertheless it does not have to cope with the really freak run or
preponderance, and the only way in which we can guarantee to

emerge victorious from such an encounter is to make provision for
wasted wins as well as for the Zero effect.

For example, in this of ten columns, Black starts off gaily winning
a dozen units in the first half-column. Given even breaks therefore,
it is likely to end with a number of bets uncleared. As these may be
quite high stakes, the danger is serious.

The only answer, therefore, if we wish to cancel the effect of these
wasted wins which in themselves fail to cancel even one loss, is to
use a cancellation or write-off for each of them. Thus, should we
win the first two coups, we need either to write off two bets later,
cancelling two losses to compensate or to make a bet which wins
enough to cancel two losses by itself.

The Extraneous 'certainty'

The best way to do this, to avoid a number of failures sending the
basic stake very high, is to use odd bets outside the normal routine,
extraneous bets placed on what appear to be certainties. Thus a
weather eye cocked at the numerical record card will from time to
time reveal that Odd or High has experienced a successful run of
perhaps eight or nine winners in succession. A serious progression
should therefore be capable of winning 1 unit and this is all we need
to compensate for a wasted bet.

It must of course be crossed off the line, not merely pocketed. Its sole
raison d'être is to shorten that line.

Large Profits; Slow Returns

Once again patience is required, but the method is attractive to the
player whose one concern is to make a profit. The staking unit will
normally be increased to two or even four times the normal. Thus if
the standard unit is normally 2/6, a stake of 10/– may be used, while
a capital of ten pounds should be sufficient.

Wait for three hypothetical bets on any even chance position; then
back the opposite, the non-dominant. If it wins, wait for the next
equivalent position.

If it loses, continue backing the same position for the same flat stake.
Not until the position shows a loss-line of eight, i.e. 1 1 1 1 1 1 1 1

is there an increase of stake. As soon as such a line is reduced to four, i.e. 1 1 1 1 *1 1 1 1* the stake returns to 1 unit.

As soon as a line is cleared, even if this occurs in two bets—one lost, one won, a fresh target is sought.

We play this against the first of our Practice Columns, p. 212.

(N) B	(R) R	
11		
	23	
22		
	1	
10		
35		
2		Spin 7 shows three for Black. Stake 1 unit Red. Wins.
	27	
	30	
	19	No. 19 gives three Red and three High. Stake 1 unit
	5	Black, 1 unit Low.
15		Low wins, Black loses. Continue 1 unit Black. This wins
	36	and cancels. Fresh target 1 unit Even. Wins with No. 36.
0		
	5	
	1	No. 1 gives target 1 unit Black.
31		Wins. Fresh target 1 unit Even.
4		Wins.
33		No. 33 gives fresh target 1 unit Red. Wins.
	34	
24		No. 24 gives fresh target 1 unit Low. Wins. Gives fresh
4		target 1 unit Odd. Wins.
	3	
29		
	19	No. 19 gives fresh target 1 unit Even. Loses. Continue
11		1 unit Even.
	34	Wins. Cancel line. Seek fresh target.
	21	
24		No. 24 gives fresh target Low.
	34	Loses. Continue 1 unit Low.
17		Wins. Cancel line. Seek fresh target.
13		
	27	No. 27 gives fresh target 1 unit Even.
28		Wins.
	7	
	21	

Result a gain of 9 units. A most satisfactory line, but plenty will be less so; frustration is a natural feature of this type of play and must be accepted if the required safety factory is to be maintained. The average profit on this type of play is not likely to be 9 units per column but more line 2 units, while it may be that two or even three columns will be played with no apparent result.

Nevertheless, provided the player is content with the limitations of this method, it must be recommended.

The Longest Haul

The patience of a Job plus a good capital turn this method into a winner. It outrages most of our normal rules however. We have shown that to use a Split Martingale in its pristine purity is as dangerous as a rattlesnake bite, yet this method uses it fearlessly. We have warned against the danger of hitting the House ceiling, but this method disregards that risk. We have shown that to play Black and Red (for example) at the same time is not really to be recommended, yet this method will undertake the task immediately the player's book-keeping becomes good enough.

It is a complicated method which requires study. The capital available should be about twice the House maximum for even chance positions. Such an amount will be needed only rarely, but if it is not available heavy losses will be encountered unnecessarily. The money must be there even if it is called upon only once in twenty sessions.

Drill

The minimum unit permitted on an even chance is divided according to the wish of the player, conforming on a sliding scale to the amount he wishes to win, the speed at which he wishes to win it, the capital he has in hand and the risk he is willing to take.

For illustrative purposes we take a casino with a minimum stake of 5/– and a maximum of £100–0–0. We decide to use as our basic, personal unit, a stake of 1/–, one-fifth of the minimum permitted. This obviously gives us a great advantage. The House limits are deliberately set so that only a certain number of positive bets is possible. By reducing the minimum stake from 5/– to 1/– we expand those limits considerably, and, should we so desire, could expand them even more, taking as our personal unit merely sixpence. And could reduce this almost to infinity—to fractions of a farthing theoretically—but might have to wait half a lifetime before winning anything at all.

Obviously, however, as the minimum stake on the table is 5/–, we cannot place anything smaller. The drill therefore is to place the minimum stake until such time as our personal loss line demands that we increase it. If we are playing in units of 1/–, we shall place—using our standard one hypothetical bet for our Split Martingale—the minimum House unit four times before we can show a loss line of *1* 1 1 1 1 on the table. Our personal line however, written in units of 1/–, will read *1* 1 2 3 4 and the next stake required will be 5 units. Desiring to show a profit, this will require a House unit stake of 10/–. Good book-keeping is necessary. The personal line is given in the example column as (*a*). The standard Split Martingale drill is followed, and an increase of stake on the House line (*b*) is made when the personal stake reaches each multiple of five, e.g.

Personal line.   Units of 1/–   *1* 1 2 3 4
House line.   Units of 5/–   *1* 1 1 1 1

The personal line now requires a stake of 5 units. To make a profit if that wins, we need a stake of 2 units, House, i.e. 10/–. If this is lost, the lines will read:

(*a*) *1* 1 2 3 4 5   next stake 6
(*b*) *1* 1 1 1 1 2   next stake 2

We play a column:

We are backing RED.   (*a*) = personal line, 1/–;
(*b*) = actual stake placed, unit of 5/–
Hypothetical bet italicised *1*.

Colour wins		Lines				Next stake
B		(*a*) *1*	1			2
		(*b*) *1*	*1*			1
	R	(*a*) *1*				1
		(*b*) *1*				1

Note: The clearance of the (*a*) line by a stake of 2 units (2/–) obviously has no effect on our pocket. Only the stake actually placed can achieve that.

Colour wins	Lines				Next stake
B	(*a*) *1*	1			2
	(*b*) *1*	1			1
B	(*a*) *1*	1	2		3
	(*b*) *1*	1	1		1
B	(*a*) *1*	1	2	3	4
	(*b*) *1*	1	1	1	1

[Continued Overleaf

Continued from previous page]

Colour wins	Lines	Next stake
B	(a) 1 1 2 3 4	5
	(b) 1 1 1 1 1	2

Note: Including our hypothetical bet we have now lost the equivalent of five units. Our next stake is to show a profit if it wins.

Colour wins	Lines	Next stake
B	(a) 1 1 2 3 4 5	6
	(b) 1 1 1 1 1 2	2
B	(a) 1 1 2 3 4 5 6	7
	(b) 1 1 1 1 1 2 2	2
B	(a) 1 1 2 3 4 5 6 7	8
	(b) 1 1 1 1 1 2 2 2	2
B	(a) 1 1 2 3 4 5 6 7 8	9
	(b) 1 1 1 1 1 2 2 2 2	2
B	(a) 1 1 2 3 4 5 6 7 8 9	10
	(b) 1 1 1 1 1 2 2 2 2 2	3

Note: Split Martingale method, adding the two end figures of our personal (a) line together, a total of 10, shows that we have now expended the equivalent of two series of five, so must again increase the actual stake on the table, line (b).

Colour wins	Lines	Next stake
B	(a) 1 1 2 3 4 5 6 7 8 9 10	11
	(b) 1 1 1 1 1 2 2 2 2 2 3	3
B	(a) 1 1 2 3 4 5 6 7 8 9 10 11	12
	(b) 1 1 1 1 1 2 2 2 2 2 3 3	3
R	(a) 1 2 3 4 5 6 7 8 9 10	11
	(b) 1 1 1 1 1 2 2 2 2 2 3	3
R	(a) 2 3 4 5 6 7 8 9	11
	(b) 1 1 1 1 1 2 2 2 2	3
R	(a) 3 4 5 6 7 8	11
	(b) 1 1 1 1 2 2 2 2	3
R	(a) 4 5 6 7	11
	(b) 1 1 1 2 2 2	3
B	(a) 4 5 6 7 11	15
	(b) 1 1 1 2 2 2 3	4
R	(a) 5 6 7	12
	(b) 1 1 2 2 2	3
B	(a) 5 6 7 12	17
	(b) 1 1 2 2 2 3	4
B	(a) 5 6 7 12 17	22
	(b) 1 1 2 2 2 3 4	5
R	(a) 6 7 12	18
	(b) 1 2 2 2 3	4
B	(a) 6 7 12 18	24
	(b) 1 2 2 2 3 4	5

Colour wins	Lines							Next stake
B	(a) 6	7	12	18	24			30
	(b) 1	2	2	2	3	4	5	7
R	(a) 7	12	18					25
	(b) 2	2	2	3	4			6
R	(a) 12							12
	(b) 2	2	3					3
R	(a) clear							1
	(b) 2	2						1
R	(a) clear							1
	(b) 1	2						1

The lack of co-ordination between the lengths of the respective lines is inevitable when they consist of different stakes. When the House line is clear, the profit will have been 1 unit, House, i.e. the initial hypothetical bet in the line.

This seems to be a lot of work for five shillings but here we are not playing to win; we are playing not to lose; not to permit our stake to exceed the maximum. Backing Black instead of Red we would have won 13 units (House) with an outstanding line of 3 units, House. Backing both colours we could write-off an outstanding amount from the losing column against the gain on the winning column.

The capital employed in this series has been deceptively small, a mere 24 units, House. But the larger capital must be available. We use this type of line to be able to remain below the House maximum, a ceiling far too low for the dangerous Split Martingale.

Were we using the standard stake we would expect to burst through that ceiling not infrequently. Thus if the House maximum is £100–0–0 we must expect to encounter betting requirements in excess of that if we use House stakes. And, most important to consider, is that once we reach such a level, nothing is easier than to reach a far higher level. Thus, should we place a bet of £100–0–0 and be permitted to double-up, three immediate losers would require a fresh stake of £800–0–0. The wheel is just as likely to produce three losers as three winners. This then is the type of position which threatens when we use a Split Martingale, and to divide (roughly) our stake by five (or ten, or what you will) inevitably will need a really large stake from time to time. To illustrate this we return to our series and note that the last bet on the personal line was 30 units. Two losses, one win and then two more losses—a quite normal series—would have turned that line into 18 30 48 76 and a similar set following would have made it

30 48 76 94 124 154. A little see-sawing with wins and losses against an adverse preponderance may easily find us left with a first figure of 124 in the line instead of 30, and now the stake really starts to climb.

Therefore a good capital is essential if this method is to be employed. But it is inherently a winner for all that.

Backing Two Positions in Combination

From time to time we may glance down a column in play and notice that a couple of positions in combination have not appeared for some time. Positions in combination are:

Red with High, Low, Odd or Even.
Black with High, Low, Odd or Even.
High with Odd or Even.
Low with Odd or Even.

Should one or more of these be missing, an automatic, hypothetical bet position has been created and we may take advantage of it.

Drill

Stake 1 unit on each position.
After a loss, stake 2 units.
After another loss, stake 4 units.
Hypothetical requirements: four hypothetical bets should be used. Thus, if Black and Odd is the target, Red and Even must have appeared four times since the target appeared.
There will naturally be a number of stand-off bets in this play, e.g. we are backing Black and Odd; if numbers Red and Odd or Black and Even appear the bets are a stand-off, one losing, one winning.

The Lot

If it is desired to concentrate upon this type of bet—and this has much to be said for it—while some difficulty is experienced in reading the normal casino card, a special card may be prepared with six double columns. (The casino card may be used by including the margins as columns.)

The Union Jack method of notation may be employed so that targets may be immediately and automatically spotted. Each opposing pair is considered separately. The specimen diagram gives each spin as it appears, gradually building the picture through the notation.

Legend: BE = Black and Even win on the same spin.
            RO = Red and Odd do similarly.
            BO = Black and Odd.
            RE = Red and Even.
            BH = Black and High.
            RL = Red and Low.
            BL = Black and Low.
            RH = Red and High.
            HO = High and Odd.
            LE = Low and Even.
            HE = High and Even.
            LO = Low and Odd.

A

Spin

B	R
11	
	23
13	
2	
6	

Black, Odd and Low win the first spin. The pro-forma will appear:

B

BE	RO	BO	RE	BH	RL	BL	RH	HO	LE	HE	LO
		—				—					—

No. 23, Red, Odd and High wins the second spin, and the pro-forma is given a line under Red and High, (RH) Red and Odd, (RO) High and Odd (HO). The result, combined with the notation used for the first spin, produces:

C

BE	RO	BO	RE	BH	RL	BL	RH	HO	LE	HE	LO
	—	—				—	—	—			—

Note that RH has now superseded its opposite, BL.

The next three spins are won respectively, by
Black, Low, Odd; and Black, Low, Even (twice).
The pro-forma appears:

D

BE	RO	BO	RE	BH	RL	BL	RH	HO	LE	HE	LO
—		⌐				—	—	—		⌐	⌐

Black–Low has now won three times since its opposite appeared and
one more will give us four hypothetical bets which will be shown by a
line at the bottom completing a square. If more hypothetical bets are
desired they are shown by drawing diagonals across the square as in
a Union Jack.

One card, marked in this fashion, will probably last for a full
session. Numbers of course are not written at all. They are here
merely to simplify the drill.

Combinations every Spin

While the doubles above are given with a basic progression of 1 2 4
(each), and may extend their range with a second line or more, such
as 2 4 8, 3 6 12, to play this way every spin of the wheel basically
requires a single progression: 1 2 4 8 16 32.

Nevertheless a Split Martingale or Doubly Split Martingale may be
employed: 1 2 4 6 8 10 12 etc. crossing off two losses for each win,
or as before: 1 2 4, then 2 4 8, then 3 6 12 or any intermediate type
of line decided upon according to ambition and available capital.

Drill

Select a target from the first number that appears. Above, this was
No. 11 so the target may be Red and Even, Red and High, or High
and Even.

Play this target until the limit of the progression is reached or a win
is recorded. Having reached that point—say we chose Red and High,
this would be on the first spin—a fresh target is selected from the

present number, i.e. No. 23, but this will not be a reversion to the previous Black and Low, but perhaps to Black and Even or Low and Even.

This is a pretty good method and its simplicity is perhaps deceptive.

Simple Progression on two Positions in Combination

In certain continental casinos—unfortunately we have not seen this bet conceded in England—it is possible to back two even chances in combination by placing the stake on the line dividing them. This of course strictly limits the bets available. The even chances are on opposite sides of the table:

Rouge	Impair	Manque
Noir	Pair	Passe

Thus these bets may be made only on the combinations:

> Rouge–Impair.
> Impair–Manque.
> Noir–Pair.
> Pair–Passe.

On an American type table the even chances are set:[*]
Low Odd Red Black Even High
If the bet is permitted—doubtful—the available positions are therefore:

> Low–Odd.
> Odd–Red.
> Black–Even.
> Even–High.

The bet is at *even money* in contrast to the bet placed across two dozens or two columns. It is lost when both positions lose; won when both positions win; left in place when one wins and one loses. Once this obtains there is obviously no need to place a stake higher than the minimum, no division of stake being required as with dozens or columns. So, starting with 1 unit, a progression of the most simple kind may be employed, using insurance or under insurance, Martin-

[*] Manufacturers are not always in conformity.

gale or Split Martingale etc. just as with a normal 1 unit bet on any of the regular positions.

Systems of Betting on Future Runs

Once a run of any length has appeared it is not unlikely that further runs will come. This type of system can in such circumstances be extremely profitable.

Drill

Select two opposites in even chance positions. For convenience we will choose Black and Red. Place 1 unit on each. Replace the lost unit but leave the winning one to ride, playing for a series of six winners, but *not necessarily consecutive*. The method succeeds when a run of six is encountered as long as interposition by the opposite does not exceed one spin and provided that the fifth spin does not lose.

(N)	(R)
B	R
	9
15	
	21
	12
0	
2	
	18
	23
	7

Theoretically 1 unit is placed upon both Black and Red for the first spin. This is of course somewhat superfluous and strictly technically one should not bet at all but await the outcome and place the 2 units on the winner. The technical point is that a Zero effect is avoided for that spin. No subsequent spin is affected unless a win is made.

Red wins the first spin and shows 2 units. The lost unit on Black is replaced. Black wins the next. The lost 2 units on Red are replaced. This replacement is done only once consecutively. Should this 2 units be lost, Black winning again, the stake reverts to 1 unit. Such replacement for one spin however may be repeated later in the same sequence—as it in fact is here.

Red wins with No. 21, showing 4 units now, while the 2 unit loss on Black is replaced. Red wins with No. 12, and shows 8 units. The lost unit on Black is replaced. Zero wins. Both stakes are imprisoned. Black is liberated, Red is lost. The 8 units lost on Red are replaced— for one spin only. Red wins, and now shows 16 units. The lost unit on Black is replaced. Red wins the next two spins with Nos. 23 and 7. There are now 64 units showing on Red. These are lifted.

Balance

Black has cost 6 units. Red has cost 1 single unit at Spin 1, 2 units after Spin 2, 8 units after Spin 6; a total of 17 units outlay against a lift of 64 units, i.e. a direct profit of 47 units.

Replacements may be higher and so more costly, but the maximum replacement admitted is 16. Should a bet of 32 units lose it is not replaced but reversion made at once to the single unit. It is true that replacement may produce a win of 64 but it can also produce a loss of 32, while the win of 64 is no more, 32 of it being our own money. The replacement of a 32 is barred basically because there remains only one spin to complete the series, and so 32 can only double itself whereas a bet of 16 may quadruple itself.

The method is a genuine gamble, capable of making a large profit quickly. It may also require a good-sized capital if the required length of run fails to materialise. It will happen that a long series of near misses occurs before a short burst of three or four quick wins turns the whole scene inside out and a large loss becomes a large profit.

The same principle may be used for runs of fewer wins, taking 32 units off after a successful run of five, 16 units after a run of four, etc.

Going with the wheel

A similar type of play with perhaps slightly more initial justification is to base such a method on the immediate prior showing of the wheel.

Thus when a run of five or six appears, the dominant colour is backed to produce a run of four, three only counting towards profit.

(N)	(R)
B	R
33	
6	
4	
17	
31	
	18
11	
	19
	36
	3
	27
	9

A run of five appears. It is decided to play for a run of four to appear. The change in colour is awaited; when Black ceases to win, Red showing, Red is backed for 1 unit. This loses. The dominant is now Black, so 1 unit is placed on Black. This loses so 1 unit is placed on the fresh dominant, Red. This is permitted to run for three spins, all of which win. 8 units are lifted against an outlay of 3 units, showing a profit of 5 units. Note the bet is lifted regardless of the fact that the run may continue. It might not.

Note: this method backs the dominant, as opposed to the previous method which backed both sides simultaneously.

A run of five is the minimum which should be accepted in order to back a run to produce four, three valid. Should the above run on Red have changed after four wins, the method should be abandoned until a further run of five appears. As it shows at present we may persist in looking for another run of four.

High Play at Half-Price

This is a staking-plan which cannot but prove attractive to players with a mild mathematical bent, small money and the desire to play for high stakes.

A saving bet is placed on the opposite position to the one backed. It is placed at a chosen point in the line, according to the risk considered worth accepting and the amount desired to be saved. The saving bet should produce as near as possible to totality of saving.

A mild shorthand for the illustration of this is desirable. The basic line will be written as usual, 1 2 4 etc. (or whatever line may be chosen. Insurance bets may be included if desired at any point).

A saver on Bet No. 2 of 1 unit will be written:

Saver		1
Basic line	1	2

The amount this will save should the basic line bet lose, will be shown above once more, as:

May be lifted		2 if Bet No. 2 loses.
Saver		1
Basic line	1	2

The above display therefore indicates that we have lost Bet No. 1 for 1 unit and have just placed Bet No. 2 for 2 units and also a saver on the opposite position (Black if we are backing Red etc.) of 1 unit; and that, should Bet No. 2 lose, we may, if we wish, lift 2 units as a saver from the opposite position.

We decide to leave the saver after having lost Bet No. 2, so the display becomes:

$$\begin{array}{ccc} & 2 & 4 \\ & 1 & \\ 1 & 2 & 4 \end{array}$$

Bet No. 3 has been placed, the saver remaining untouched. If Bet No. 3 wins, the entire line is cleared. If it loses, 4 units may be lifted as a saver and the line will become 1 1 2. Having got so far we may replace our bet of 4 units and, using the same 50% of saving, place a fresh saving bet of 2 units, giving:

$$4$$
$$2$$
$$1 \quad 1 \quad 2 \quad 4$$

If this Bet No. 4 wins the line becomes 1 1. If it loses, we place another bet of, say, 6 units—Split Martingale category—leave the saver and produce:

$$4 \quad 8$$
$$2$$
$$1 \quad 1 \quad 2 \quad 4 \quad 6$$

If this Bet No. 5 of 6 units wins the line becomes once more 1 1 2. If it loses, the line becomes 1 1 2 4 6 which is fair enough for having lost five successive bets. The Standard Martingale line at this stage would have read 1 2 4 8 16 a loss of 31 units against the present 14 units—plus of course the saver which has cost us 2 units; our total outlay being therefore 16 units but against which we can retrieve 8 units simply by picking up our saver. So, in practice, these five lost bets can be accepted at a cost of 8 units and a fresh start made. The only difference in favour of the Martingale is that it would have won 1 unit had any one of its bets won whereas our own line wins 1 unit only on the very first bet. In our favour is the tremendous saving of capital outlay, we being able to place a bet now of 8 units or 10 units while the Martingale requires 32 units which may have to be followed by 64 units and so on.

Better Practice

The above skeleton of the principle of saving specific percentages of capital outlay shows that, properly manipulated, a line of consecutive losers may prove very far from costly.

However we do want to win. Therefore some degree of loss should be accepted in order to facilitate this a little more. The normal adverse run is likely to prove extremely expensive. We can hardly demand that we make a profit against it as well as on all the favourable runs. So, should things go badly, we should be prepared to accept a modicum of immediate loss.

Let us therefore play our standard Martingale for the first three bets 1 2 4 giving us a win of 1 unit if any of these bets wins. After that, as danger may be in the offing, we may embark upon some drastic saving. What is needed is a size of stake and saving bet which will see the winning bet reduce the line and the saving bet prevent an increased loss. A tall order perhaps. We try.

To be lifted if Bet No. 4				10 loses
Saver			5	
Basic line	1	2	4	6

Here we have lost three bets in succession, so place a saver which will save an immediate 80% of outlay.

A. If the natural bet wins the line is reduced by 1 unit.
B. If the natural bet loses the line is increased by 1 unit. We take it that the natural bet has lost, for otherwise we would simply reduce the line by 1 unit and repeat the previous bet, as above, reducing the loss by 1 unit each time it won.

We take it therefore that the natural bet has lost. We leave the saving bet and stake a fresh bet at No. 5 of 8 units, Split Martingale standard stake.

If you win, you Win; if you Lose—you also win

To be lifted if				10	20 Bet No. 5 loses.
Saver			5		
Basic line	1	2	4	6	8

A. If this bet wins the line is reduced accordingly.
B. If it loses the line becomes 1 2 3 by lifting no less than 20 units from the saver.

Thus we have produced a type of bet which must win whether it wins or loses. This seems to be a desirable situation.

The permutation addict will of course be able to play around with this sort of thing for hours, producing lines to make large wins for every loss and small losses for every win if he feels slightly perverse. But here the method needs no elaboration; anyone interested will inevitably have pen and paper in hand already.

The Zero danger

Zero winning against this kind of stake-manipulation might appear
somewhat annoying, but it is not too bad. For example, should Zero
win when we have placed the last bet above, No. 5, both stakes will
be imprisoned. If we wish to take a chance we may, but it must be
remembered that one of those bets is inevitably going to be lost
because they are direct opposites.

The best drill is to *share both*. Here we then lift 9 units, conceding a
loss of—in practice—4 units and leaving the line 1 2 4 4 6. Zero of
course came a little early; it would have done better to delay for a
spin or so. Delaying one spin would have seen:

$$10 \quad 20 \quad 40$$
$$5$$
$$1 \quad 2 \quad 4 \quad 6 \quad 8 \quad 14 \text{ (say)}$$

Now if Zero wins, stakes of 14 and 20 are imprisoned and a share of
them gives us 17 units to lift. Delayed one spin more would have
seen:

$$10 \quad 20 \quad 40 \quad 80$$
$$5$$
$$1 \quad 2 \quad 4 \quad 6 \quad 8 \quad 14 \quad 32 \text{ (say)}$$

This is a happy position after losing six consecutive bets. If our 32
units bet wins the line comes right down to 1 1 2 4 while if it
should lose we may take 80 units from the saver, clear the entire line
and take a profit of 8 units, fair enough for losing seven successive
bets.

But Zero wins. We share the imprisoned stakes of 32 and 40 for a lift
of 36 units. So even Zero produces a profit. Summary here:

If basic line bets wins, we win 32 units.
If it loses we win 48 units.
If Zero wins we win 4 units.

Colloquially this is known as getting it coming, going *and* sideways.
What is more, the situation improves the longer Zero holds off. If we
lose this bet of 32 units and place one of 64 units, Zero now winning,
the summary is:

We win: we win 64 units.
We lose: we win 96 units.
Zero wins: we win 8 units.

Yet no matter how materially satisfactory such a result may be, it is far from being aesthetically so. Where is the sense of artistry, the appreciation of the harmony of numbers? It would be no less than barbaric to refrain from placing an odd chip of Zero at such a moment. It is an extra chip, true, but it does not go into the day-book; its place in our records is in the Zero personal p & l account. But even were it a genuine sacrifice it cannot be a high price to pay for the favour of the Muse. Here then is the aesthetic, the harmonious play:

$$10 \quad 20 \quad 40 \quad 80$$
$$5$$
$$1 \quad 2 \quad 4 \quad 6 \quad 8 \quad 14 \quad 40$$
and 1 unit on Zero.

If Red wins we win 39 units. (Lifting 80 units from Red including our stake of 40, but losing 1 unit on Zero.)

If Black wins we win 39 units. (Losing our 40 units on Red and 1 unit on Zero, but lifting 80 units from Black.)

If Zero wins we win 35 units. (Lifting 36 units from Zero, including our 1 unit stake; sharing 80 units imprisoned, 40 on Red, 40 on Black, exactly compensating for the 40 units we placed on Red.)

And the croupier may be notified in advance.

Flat Stake Play

There are a number of standard bets and variations on these which are regularly employed by many players. Flat stake play technically means that the stake is unvarying, but it is quite possible to engineer a sequence or progression in the stake in order to increase the chances of winning. Basically one main section of flat stake play attempts to turn the *immediate* odds in favour of the player. This is easy enough. The wheel is not concerned with the amount of money staked, so for immediate play, the natural factor of mechanical odds multiplied by money at risk does not apply; all that counts is the odds.

The obvious way to win 1 unit, having tremendous immediate odds in favour of the player, is to back 35 numbers. If one of them wins, 35 units are won, 34 units are lost. This is an almost sure way to obtain the fare for the taxi home. Sometimes however it must lose. Over an extended period—on average—it will lose precisely what the wheel demands—1 unit in every 37 staked. But the player is not concerned with long periods but with immediate plays. He will surmount the disaster hurdle when he comes to it.

Covering 32 numbers

This is a standard play. 1 unit is placed on Red, 2 units across the first and second columns. Both bets may be lost only if one of the numbers 0, 6, 15, 24 or 33 wins. These comprise the Zero plus four Black numbers in the third column. If a Red number in the third column wins, 1 unit is lost. There are eight of these numbers. But there are ten Red numbers in the first two columns. Should one of these win, both bets win. Should a Black number win, the result is all square.

Black plus First and Third Columns

The same bet is to be found using Black and the first and third columns (1 unit on each of these). There are only four Red numbers in the central column, and these, plus the Zero, are the only numbers which can cause both bets to be lost.

The play should be made for a set period, an amount to be won decided beforehand, a certain number of spins played. The target should be in the region of 5 units and play should cease when this has been won.

Selection

The preponderance should be reviewed before selecting which of these two identical bets is to be placed. If the wheel seems to be favouring Black for the present, choose the second; if Red, the first.

Manque and the Sixain 19–24. Passe and the Sixain 13–18.

These are again standard bets and are dealt with in the section on 'Two Dozens'.

Progression on the Colour and Two Columns

The straight Martingale line would be:

Colour	Column	Column
1	1	1
2	2	2
4	4	4
8	8	8
16	16	16
32	32	32

This requires a capital of 189 units.

Split Martingale

1	1	1
2	2	2
4	4	4
6	6	6
8	8	8
10	10	10
12	12	12

This requires 129 units.

The Split Martingale is of course unable to include any stake which comprises an uneven number of units because of the fact that the bet must be divided between two columns equally.

It may be done if the unit is not of the smallest denomination available. Thus if the smallest chip is 5/– and the unit chosen is 10/– a bet of 1 unit may be placed across two columns. This will necessitate the stake on the colour being reduced to half-a-unit, 5/–.

Should 1 unit be placed on the colour (10/–) the bet across the columns must be 2 units. It can never be 3 units unless the colour again deals in half-units. If the unit chosen is the smallest, 3 units can never be placed across the columns.

Capital

The capital for the Split Martingale is set at 129 units but it must be recalled that the double loss can only occur when one of five particular numbers wins. Thus the entire capital will rarely be required and even more rarely be endangered.

Simple Flat-stake plays

Place 2 units on Passe; 1 unit on the first dozen. This breaks even when the dozen wins, theoretically one-third of the time; wins 1 unit if Passe wins, theoretically one-half of the time; loses 3 units to Zero and the sixain 13–18, theoretically approximately one-sixth of the time.

This method covers, bar the Zero, 30 numbers out of 36, breaks even on 12, wins 1 unit on 18 of them. *The Opposite* is of course: 2 units on Manque, 1 unit on the top dozen, losing only to Zero and the sixain 19–24.

Progression

Starting with this small outlay it is not unreasonable to build a progression upon these 30 numbers. They should be given a chance to succeed over a period before an increase of stake is made. Nine spins is about right. This gives a prospective gain of 1 unit per nine spins, not over-optimistic when basic odds are 5–1 in favour of not losing, even money to win. Nine spins gives four 'sessions' per column, which, in favourable circumstances, produces a profit of 4 units per column. This is about the right amount. It does not sound much but a steady profit of 4 units per column is the hard grafter's idea of systemic perfection. 10 units per hour, 30 units for session. Excellent wages.

Hypothetical bets

Before deciding whether to back Passe and the first dozen or Manque and the third dozen it is not without value to check how the wheel is performing. A few wins for High do not necessarily suggest that we back Low, but rather suggest that a preponderance prevails for High and that therefore is the right target. A few wins for either the first or third dozen however may be considered to be hypothetical bets, and the target chosen accordingly.

A point to remember is that, having chosen well and pocketed a number of wins, there actually have been present a number of hypothetical bets for our present position, so that it may be good policy to consider a change to the other.

The block of numbers containing so many first dozen wins should be kept in mind also. We do not desire to suffer because of these if we are using a progression. With a flat stake it is immaterial, because the favourable swings from the larger arc of the wheel will naturally counterbalance the unfavourable ones from the minor arc; but when using a progression it is advisable to give some bias to the choice of the first dozen.

Multifarious

Personal flat-stake plays abound, and are known individually as Le Jeu, (the game), e.g. a player will invariably stake a chip on Quatre premiers, one on the carre 25–29 and one each en plein 12, 17 and 22. This has no meaning and is just as likely to be based upon the family birthday dates as upon anything else. Once the player has asked for his 'jeu' to be set a few times the croupier will set it auto-

matically, either on receipt of the necessary chips or out of winnings
before paying the residue.

Single Numbers—short sections

Experience tends to teach that once a number has repeated itself
immediately another number is likely to do so in the near future.
Advantage may therefore sometimes be taken of this.
The situation is not the same as with Les Voisins, where the croupier
'has fallen' into a rhythm, because these are alternate spins. It simply
indicates that the croupier has struck a spin which travels just about a
precise number of revolutions and so is likely to end where it started
on the wheel.

Drill

Back the next four numbers to appear for four spins each. Alternatively, the next three numbers, or the next two numbers for six spins
each. The number of spins etc. must be at the discretion of the player
in proportion to his capital and ambition. Once the section fails,
abandon it and wait until another number repeats itself immediately.
A progression may now be started, using a 2 unit stake.

The Zero

Frequently a session of some length is found without the occurrence
of a Zero. This strongly suggests that the Les Voisins theory is
working, and that the croupier has fallen into a rhythm which has
caused him to omit the Zero section of the wheel. A quick check may
be made on this by glancing down the columns to note if Zero's
neighbours have won their share. The important numbers are 26 and
32. If they also appear infrequently, there may be a chance to back
Zero soon.
This will occur after a change of croupiers. The relief man will arrive
after perhaps half-an-hour or an hour according to the working rota.
Now, should he produce a Zero, experience shows that he is likely to
do it again soon.

A unit should therefore be placed on Zero and repeated each spin. The length of time allotted to permitted failure is at the discretion of the player. But it must be remembered that even if no success is obtained, the result is not utter loss. When keeping records the profit and loss account for the Zero should always be kept separately. This present loss—if it is one—will simply go into that account. Over a period the player should win his prescribed average or somewhere near it, and these lost spins will therefore be doing their share of the negative work.

The point is that here is a very favourable situation for a recurrence of Zero. If we are backing Zero, now is the time to do it. The p and l account may then over a period show a surprisingly high percentage of gain.

Progression

Minor progressions may be initiated on these Zero bets, but, as always with single numbers, may be protracted while requiring a reasonably large capital. Nevertheless, any monotony present in the normal single number progression may be avoided with the Zero, this progression being split over a number of different sessions, each time being employed only when circumstances suggest that they are favourable.

The shift worked by the croupier who failed to produce a Zero will of course provide us with automatic sleeping-time.

Columns versus Dozens

Backing two columns is open to the accusation that faced the backing of two dozens across the dozens dividing line, i.e. that the Zero effect is dangerous. This was largely circumvented when backing two dozens by the manipulation of stakes, using Passe or Manque plus the adjacent sixain, and thus ensuring a save of three-eights of the total stake each time Zero won.

This cannot be done with columns. No positions exist which can take care of two columns in this manner. Nevertheless there is a strong argument in favour of using two columns in preference to two dozens. For this we need a diagram of the wheel.

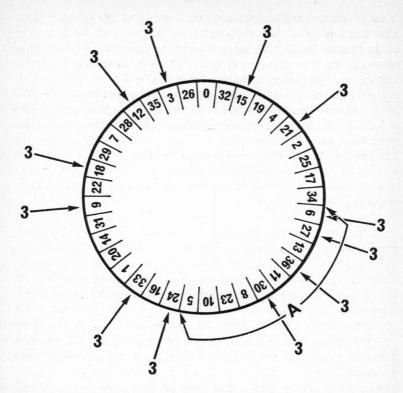

Examining that diagram we note that the numbers multiples of three and therefore appearing in the third column are extremely evenly spaced around the wheel. No block of such numbers exists and only two of them, Nos. 6 and 27 are actually juxtaposed.

This means that when playing across the first two columns no human error or fallibility will affect the result. The croupier is the only human element in the working of a Roulette wheel, and therefore his actions are the only ones which can affect a result if a result can be affected at all.

He can fall into a rhythm—inevitably must—and this may produce a series of spins resulting in favouring a particular section of the wheel. This is the premise upon which the system Les Voisins is based, and an examination of records plus experience (and records are simply experience written down) tends to justify this belief. For example when a number repeats itself immediately, it is extremely likely that another number will do the same thing very shortly. This is a reflection of rhythm.

So the distribution of the dangerous third column when we back Red plus the first two columns is not in any way unfavourable and is unlikely to be affected by human fallibility.

On the other hand we see that block of numbers marked A. Here is a group of ten numbers which contains no less than five from the first dozen. If our croupier starts to favour such a block it will undoubtedly prejudice our chances if we are betting across the top dozens, i.e. playing Passe and the sixain 13–18.

Better Odds are no Good

It is true that the massing of numbers from one particular dozen improves the odds in our favour in the larger arc of the wheel but this is no advantage. Two-thirds of the time we are certainly winning more than we by rights should, the croupier spinning completely at random, and for the other third winning less, the latter position is dangerous.

A number of single unit wins on our card may be acceptable but if the eventual price to be paid is a lost progression the combination becomes a liability. Single unit wins are good but not vital; a lost progression is not only immediately dangerous but consequently dangerous in that it may cause a second line to be lost also. This could be very expensive.

Therefore no matter which play we use on the dozens the inequality of distribution prevailing is likely to act unfavourably.

Stemming however directly from this positioning of numbers comes the system of backing the first dozen as soon as the wheel starts to favour the block 6 to 5.

The numbers may be written across the record card if no wheel-card is at hand:

$$5 \quad 6 \quad 8 \quad 10 \quad 11 \quad 13 \quad 23 \quad 27 \quad 30 \quad 36$$

Placed in natural, numerical order a single glance will be enough to show whether the winning number is there. If it is, using the rhythm theory, the first dozen may be backed, either with a flat stake or with a progression. If a progression is used it should contain some insurance.

1 1 1 1

Bets No. 1 and 2 win 2 units and 1 unit respectively. Bet No. 3 is insurance, cancelling the previous two losses, Bet No. 4 is Split Martingale in character, cancelling two out of three losing bets and leaving the line at 1.

1 1 1 1 2 2

Bet No. 5 cancels the entire line, No. 6 the previous three bets.

It is unwise to use protracted progressions on dozens, while as the present method is based upon the rhythm theory it is clearly incongruous to continue using it when the rhythm has obviously been lost. Recommended therefore is a limited line of 1 1 1 2. Should that fail, the progression should be abandoned, the line reserved for when the target is again in view. Then an increased progression may be used, as: 2 2 2 3, once again abandoning after four plays. A method such as this, using a slowly increasing stake, is a most attractive ancillary to the standard system. An adequate capital must be allotted to it.

Covering the Table

This type of play does not lend itself readily to any sort of progression unless a genuinely large capital is available.

Bets are laid on: No. 32 et chevaux or carrés,
                      23 et chevaux or carrés
                      14 et chevaux or carrés

As soon as one of these bets wins the winning position is shifted one square upwards.

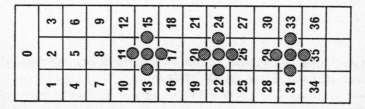

Nos. 32, 23 and 14 et chevaux. 15 units.

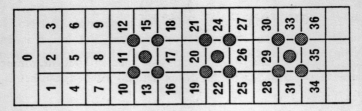

Nos. 32, 23 and 14 et carrés. 15 units.

If No. 32, 23 or 14 wins en plein the central stake is doubled, (or perhaps completed). If a side-stake wins (No. 32) No. 32's chips move to No. 29. The others remain unless 'pushed'. If one of the others wins the same drill is carried out. When a bet reaches No. 5 and scores, it moves down the table again.

A progression is not inviting on the carrés display as a single win on a carre still shows a loss. But on the chevaux display, where a win by a single cheval gains 3 units, a reasonable progression is quite feasible. Nevertheless it should not be started immediately, but the display should be set for six spins. If no profit is shown by then it may be doubled. This, carried for a further six spins, requires a capital of 270 units. An increase for a third set of six spins, using a 3 unit stake, takes this to 540 units.

The chevaux display covers fifteen numbers, so—on average—should produce a win some 40% of the time.

Covering 30 numbers

This is a reasonable flat stake play provided we cease to regard it as purely flat stake but include a gradual progression.

Drill

Stake 1 unit on Manque, 1 unit on the 3rd dozen. Alternatively: 1 unit on Passe, 1 unit on the 1st dozen.

Loss
Zero plus the numbers 19–24 produce a loss of 2 units.

Gain

1 unit is won each time the 3rd dozen wins.

Equal

When the even chance, Manque or Passe wins without the winning number being included in the dozen actually backed, the bet is a stand-off.

Progression

When the line reaches 10 units, (2 2 2 2 2) the stake is increased to 2 units on each position. Each win now clears one loss. The loss mounts of course to 4 units, so the increase of stake should normally be restrained until a short series of losses have come swiftly.

The next series in the progression to clear a line of loss, better now six, 4 4 4 4 4 4 will be 4 units on each position.

This is a simple Martingale line 1 2 4. It may be lengthened 1 2 4 8 16, changed to a Split Martingale 1 2 4 6 8 etc. or to a series of abbreviated lines as 1 2 4; 2 4 6; 3 5 8 etc. or any alternative series which meets the player's requirements, including whatever amount of insurance or under-insurance he cares to incorporate.

Covering 36 numbers

This is a popular flat-stake series.

1 unit on Manque
1 unit on 3rd dozen
1 unit on 1st column
1 unit on the carré 20–24.

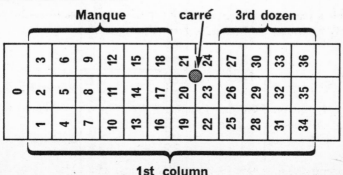

It will be seen that this display covers the entire table with the exception of the Zero. The outlay is 4 units per spin and certain numbers are duplicated, i.e. those which are in both Manque (Low) and in the first column, Nos. 1, 4, 7, 10, 13, 16, and those which are in both the last dozen and the first column, Nos. 25, 28, 31, 34.

Loss
If the winning number is in Manque and also in the second or third column the loss is 2 units.
If the winning number is 19 or 22 in the first column the loss is 1 unit.
If the winning number is in the second or third column, in the top dozen but not in the carré the loss is 1 unit.
If Zero wins the loss is 4 units.

Gain
If the winning number is in Manque and the first column the gain is 1 unit.

If the winning number is 25, 28, 31 or 34 the gain is 2 units.
If the winning number is in the carré the gain is 5 units.

This is better panoramically comprehended through a numbers diagram.

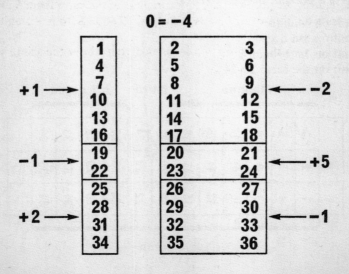

Covering 37 numbers

A 'saver' may be placed on Zero, thus covering the entire table. This naturally reduces the gain or increases the loss by 1 unit when a positive number wins, but produces 35 units (31 units profit) when Zero wins. If this is undertaken therefore the record should, as usual, be kept separately, the score for Zero being placed in the Zero p and l account.

Permutation

This layout may of course be permuted; it is a kindergarten jig-saw and the simple opposite is:

1 unit on 1st dozen
1 unit Passe (High)
1 unit 3rd column
1 unit the carré 13–17.

The Sixain

It is reasonable to use the sixain 19–24 instead of the carré 20–24. This reduces the profit on the four numbers in the carré from 5 units to 2 units but improves the result on Nos. 19 and 22 from −1 unit to +5 units.

With the opposite permutation as immediately above the sixain will be 13–18.

How to use the Practice Columns

Cover the column with a card. Slide it down to reveal one number at a time. According to the system you have selected to use, make your bet. Uncover the next number and mark the result in your system line. This is best done on the card itself.

The columns need not be played in rotation once they have become slightly familiar. Any order is convenient, while they can be played backwards or upside down for variation.

Play each column using different systems. Add an ancillary method to the main system eventually selected. Add another. Keep the possible ancillary bets always fresh in the mind so that the positions are recognised when they occur.

Practice recording the single numbers in a marginal space; the dozens; the columns. These are records of actual play but it does not matter in what order we play them; they might have come in such an order. Records are simply experience written down and every lesson we can draw from such experience adds to our own.

Practice Columns

1		2		3		4		5	
(N) B	(R) R	(N) B	(R) R	(N) B	(R) R	(N) B	(R) R	(N) B	(R) R
11		31		24		24		35	
	23		12		19		5	29	
22			34	26			32		32
	1		16		18	29			9
10			9		5	33		29	
35			23	35		26		31	
2			3	2		17			19
	27	10		26		13		26	
	30	2		8			32	6	
	19	11		26			25		25
	5		19	28			3	17	
15		28		20			25	15	

1 (N) B	1 (R) R	2 (N) B	2 (R) R	3 (N) B	3 (R) R	4 (N) B	4 (R) R	5 (N) B	5 (R) R
	36		25	17			8		7
0		15		10		31		8	
	5		1	11			3		9
	1	29		6			25		30
31		19		29		8			34
4		27			36	31		28	
33		5		8			3	24	
	34	31			19	2		2	
24		36		22		35			23
4		8			19	26			32
	3	18		20		28			1
29		4			14		1	29	
	19	15			9		16	17	
11		31		22			16		18
	34	6		20			16		19
	21		7	11		31		29	
24			5		27	20		2	
	34	10			7		36	2	
17		30			32	33		26	
13		8			18	35		20	
	27		16	28			36		32
28		22			12	23		17	
	7		1		23	11		20	
	21		5	11			30	13	
		10			21		5		5

Spin 37 not
played. Not
recorded

6 (N) B	6 (R) R	7 (N) B	7 (R) R	8 (N) B	8 (R) R	9 (N) B	9 (R) R	10 (N) B	10 (R) R
29		22			12		6		32
13		15			1		11	11	
13			9	31		15		15	
	30		36		9	13		20	
13			21		36		5	33	
24			5		27		14		7
8		29		17			12		34
	36		9	2			12		7
	32		32	24		33		4	
	19	10		8		31		26	
15			34	6			19		3
33			36	33			3	0	

[Continued Overleaf

Continued from previous page]

6		7		8		9		10	
(N)	(R)	(N)	(R)	(N)	(R)	(N)	(R)	(N)	(R)
B	R	B	R	B	R	B	R	B	R
15			25		19		25	8	
31		20			18	4		6	
22		11			34		25	15	
28			19	22		2			16
	27		30	35			1	8	
	12	22			1		16		9
	7	22		8			25		21
	12		34	17			12		18
24		28			16		24	20	
	23	6		26			23	31	
	7	0			14		28		18
17			18		12		16		1
	25	0		33			12		14
31		35			21		19	17	
	34		1		34		3		18
	5		7		34	15			5
24		31			5		7	13	
29			32		14		3		14
8		24		15		33			1
	3		3		16	8		11	
	25	31			36		34	0	
17		11			18	24			12
	1	0		26		6			36
15		29		9		17		2	
11		15		29			25	10	

The Hard Grafter at Work

(N) (R)

B R We accompany the hard grafter to a casino and are permitted to read his thoughts as he plays. The Practice Columns on p. 212 are used. He starts with a basic system of backing the change after a repeat of an even chance position (p. 167) but may change to another method at any time. He starts with a staking-plan of three lines, a Martingale (abbreviated) 1 2 4, a Split Martingale (limited) 1 2 4 6 and another Martingale (which does not command our full approval because it does not fully employ the capital) of 3 5 9.

He will of course not confine himself to his one system, but use ancillary bets whenever an opportunity arises. His staking-plan may undergo change also, especially if things go not too well. He will start, for the moment, with the simplest of all staking-plans for four-timer hypothetical bets, i.e. a 1 unit single bet, converted to a Split Martingale if it loses.

11 'No bet.'

   23 'No bet.'

22 'A change to Even after two Odds gives a system bet of 1 unit on Even.'

   1 'Loses. Fresh target after two Highs. 2 units on Even.

(N) (R)
  B   R   1 unit on Low.'
 10   'Both win.'   +2

(N) (R)   *Note:* Winnings do not appear in the hard grafter's own
  B   R   record. He keeps his chips in stacks of ten, knows how
           many he bought and so is able to judge his financial
           position at a glance. He only records losses when he loses
           a complete line because the amount of his stake, apart
           from immediate cognisance, will tell him whether he is
           using the first, second or third bet etc. But we will record
           losses.
           'No. 10 wins. No system bet available,
           but there is a four-time alternation
           Red Black Red Black, so I can back
           the dominant there;
           1 unit on Black.'
 35   'It wins, and gives a four-time alterna-
           tion Even Odd Even Odd. I back there-
           fore the dominant again; also system
           bet High.   *Line*
           1 unit on Odd.   +3
           1 unit on High.'
  2   'Both lose. Ancillary bet postponed for
           the moment. System line continued;   +3)   *1* 1
           2 unit High.'
      27   'System bet wins. No further bet avail-
           able but I notice that the Even Odd
           alternation has reach a six-timer. If it
           reaches eight I'll take that ancillary
           back. No bet then this time.'   +4)   *1*

(N) (R)
  B   R
      30   'Still no bet available. Perhaps I should
           drop to three hypotheticals; maybe a
           series on the non-dominant colour
           would be right; quick change seems to
           rule there for the moment. It's early
           days however. Wait and see.'

(N) (R)
B   R

   19   'Alternation Even Odd has reached
eight; time I stepped in; I'll try for the
colour change too; it will take a six-
timer to beat me, while the maximum
up to now is a three-timer;
2 units Odd.
1 unit Black.'

    5   'Alternation ends, so my dominant
wins. Colour change loses; carry on
with that; also system bet Low after
repeat of High;   +5)   1
2 units Black.
1 unit Low.'

(N) (R)
B   R

15   'Both win. Colour change will have to
wait after that four-timer. Another
four-timer would cost me a line. I'll try
it again if Black repeats. No bet.'   +7)

   36   'System bet High and Even.
1 unit High.
1 unit Even.'

  0   'Both imprisoned.'

    5   'Both lose.   +7)   1 1
2 units High
2 units Even.'

    1   'Both lose again.   +7)   1 2 1 2
4 units High.
4 units Even.'

31   'High wins but first line is lost on
Even. Hedge the win against that. +7)   2 4
I take on the colour again if Black
repeats. Can technically go for
another High though, so will.
1 unit High.'

  4   'Loses. System bet Even. Plus colour. +7)   1 2 4
2 units High.

(N) (R) 1 unit Even.
 B   R   1 unit Red.'

(N) (R)
 B   R
 33   'High wins. Other two lose. Line
         unchanged therefore.
         2 units Even.
         1 unit Red. Keep the insurance there.'
     34 'Both win. No bet.'   +7) 4
 24   'Colour change more rapid. I'll give it
         a try. No other bet available.
         1 unit Red.'
  4   'Loses. System bet Low. Insurance bet   +7) 1 4
         Red.
         1 unit Low.
         1 unit Red.'
 33   'Both lose.   +7) 1 1 1 4
         2 units Low.
         2 units Red.'
         (Further insurance bet.)
     34 'Colour seems to be all right. I'll cut
         out the insurance bet for the next spin
         or so, and I'll hedge those results in
         case something goes wrong here. I
         don't want to lose my second line
         while I have this amount outstanding.
         Oh! I missed a bet—system bet Odd,
         but it's still going so I've gained a
         tempo for nothing.
         1 unit Odd.
         2 units Low (Hedged).
         1 unit Black.'
 24   'Just as well I hedged. That would
         have caused a 6 unit bet which might
         have gone wrong. Odd loses. Colour
         wins.   +7) 1 1 1 4 2
         4 units Low.
         2 units Odd.
         1 unit Red.'

(N)	(R)			
B	R			

4		'Low wins. Colour wins. Odd loses. I need points, so I'll do a technical repeat of Low. 1 unit Low. 1 unit Red. 4 units Odd.'	+7)	1 1 4
	3	'Very nice; the lot. System bet on Odd. 1 unit Odd. 1 unit Black.'	+7)	
29		'Again. System bet High. 1 unit High. 1 unit Red.'	+9)	
	19	'And again. Is this going too well? Watch it, especially with that colour. 1 unit Black.'	+11)	
11		'Yes. System bet Low. 1 unit Red. 1 unit Low.'	+12)	
	34	'Colour still good. Low loses. System bet Even comes in. I missed the four-timer Odds then, cost a unit. Never mind. 1 unit Black. 1 unit Even. 2 units Low.'	+12)	1
	21	'I can win the lot so I can also lose the lot. 2 units Black. 2 units Even. 4 units Low.'	+12)	1 1 1 2
24		'Breaks even, the three bets. Shall I		

(N)	(R)	
B	R	

write them all off; balance one against the other and continue with a fresh start for the loser? I should do. Score

(N) (R)
B R

is fair enough at present; ahead of my
target per column. Better hedge and
restart. It's worth an extra unit
though; get back that one I missed just
now.
2 units Low.
1 unit Red.'

34 'Colour still good; for how long, I
wonder. Better watch it; go back to an
insurance bet, I think.   +12) 1 1 2 2
4 units Low.
1 unit Black.'

17 'Better. Line nearly cleared, so I can   +12) 1
afford a technical repeat of Low.
System bet Odd.
1 unit Low.
1 unit Odd.
1 unit Red.'

13 'Two win. Insurance on the colour this
time.   +13) 1
1 unit Red.'

27 'Insurance not needed evidently. How
long will that last? Don't trust it; keep
the bet as it is. System bet High.   +13)
1 unit Black.
1 unit High.

28 'Both win. Coming to end of column.   +15)
Highly successful, about four times
my budgeted average. I'll take a
breather for a few spins and see how
the numbers have progressed.'

Note: The hard grafter's normal recording being so sketchy, he is
able to do some on the side for numbers. The reader is invited to do
this for the practice columns.

In the meantime a review of the hard grafter's method is not out of
place. His ancillary bets are italicised for recognition purposes.
His winnings are calculated by eye. His losses, except for complete

lines, are recorded mentally, and also by eye as the croupier takes them away.

We note that he is not particularly worried about backing three even chance positions at the same time. This is supposed to be bad play, taking an unnecessary risk of Zero, but the hard grafter does not bother much about Zero. At least, not until it arrives. Worrying that it might arrive could cost him far more than he could lose when it does arrive. He will take it seriously if his stake is forced to a high level. This column has been pretty easy but he will of course encounter many a bad run, and get out of it cautiously and cagily, even to the extent of using his 'nose' on the run of the wheel, deciding that this is not his day and writing-off a couple of complete lines, accepting a small loss, and going home.

We note also that there are other bets available according to which method is employed. From the First Dozen progression from p. 206 we see that No. 23, a non-first dozen member of our block of ten numbers has arrived and a progression on the first dozen could be successful enough to suggest that this croupier has fallen into a rhythm.

Simple Alembert on Black would have won 17 units but with an outstanding line 1 2 3 4; on Red would also have won 17 units with outstanding line 1 2.

Contra Alembert on Black would have lost 15 units, a result not unexpected with those quick alternations of colour. The hard grafter handled colours better than that. Contra must also show a loss on Red.

Split Martingale on Black would have won 14 units with outstanding line 1 2 but would have reached a stake of 12 units even with this quick changing of colours.

Split Martingale on Red would have won 13 units, line clear.

Any Complete Martingale would of course have won throughout, but a glance at the fourth column tells us that were it less than a 13-bet series one entire capital could have been lost. In any event the psychological pressure engendered by the complete Martingale is too heavy for most of us. Playing a 5/- stake that 12-timer would have seen us losing £31–15–0 after Spin 11, even using four hypothetical bets, and now being forced to stake another £32 on a straight even chance, the final gain, if we win, being still a mere 5/-.

Gamblers Book Services

The one-stop mail order company for all your gambling book, video & software requirements.

Free catalogue of over 400 items on all aspects of gambling available - just write to G.B.S. (Dept HTWR), 18 Coleswood Rd, Harpenden, Herts, AL5 1EQ, England or contact us on Phone/Fax no. (0582) 761264 during normal business hours.

All orders should be paid for in Pounds Sterling. Add 10% P&P for U.K., 15% for Europe and 20% elsewhere. Credit cards (Access & Visa) are welcome and we also accept "Switch" debit cards.

We have extensive contacts throughout the world and we will endeavour to get any gambling title that is in print from anywhere in the world - just ring or write.

Listed below are a selection of our titles on Roulette.

THIRTEEN AGAINST THE BANK - Norman Leigh - £5-95 - 240 pages paperback. The classic story of the men who broke the bank. A detailed and compulsive account of how Leigh systematically won large sums of money and was banned by every French casino.

WIN AT ROULETTE - Gordon Cromwell - £4-95 - 84 pages paperback. British bias. Contents include rules & bets available, number systems, staking systems, money management, practice sessions.

ROULETTE ROUGE ET NOIR - £2-95 - 64 pages. 25000 Black & red decisions.

ROULETTE BY THE DOZENS - £2-95 - 64 pages. 25000 Columns & dozens.

ROULETTE BY THE NUMBERS - £2-95 - 64 pages. 25000 numbers.

THE NEWTONIAN CASINO - Thomas Bass - £5-99 - 320 pages paperback. Amazing true story about how a group of young physicists won at the game with the aid of a computer.

Books on other gambling subjects:

THE BIGGEST GAME IN TOWN - Al Alvarez - £5-95 - 192 pages paperback. Classic account of world poker championships - stunningly well reviewed and well written. A must for all poker fans and serious players.

THE EDUCATION OF A POKER PLAYER - Herbert Yardley - £5-95 - 160 pages paperback. Classic autobiography which is still out on its own as a poker playing manual for all levels.

WIN AT BLACKJACK - Gordon Cromwell - £4-95 - 84 pages paperback. Contents include rules, response to every situation (basic strategy), moving percentages in your favour by using basic strategy, card counting and money management.

BEAT THE DEALER - Edward Thorp - £7-95 - 220 pages paperback. A classic first published in 1962 that has now sold over 500,000 copies! and expounded the Basic strategy for the first time.

MILLION DOLLAR BLACKJACK - Ken Uston - £14-95 - 330 pages paperback - A must for any serious poker player.

SUCCESS ON THE POOLS - Simon Carrley - £4-99 - 160 pages paperback. Based on 22 years analysis of score draws.

THE NEW EXPERT HANDICAPPERS - James Quinn - £22-95 - 288 pages hardcover. Fascinating analysis of 14 top U.S. horse race handicappers and their various methods. Also includes an account of winning season with 3 of the top pro's. Of interest to serious punter.

RACING WITH A POCKET CALCULATOR - John White - £3-50 - 96 pages paperback. Analysis of form using a pocket calculator to show which races to bet on, evaluate the odds and converting the performance data into a simple points system to give you your best bet.

THE CINCINNATI KID - Richard Jessup - £6-95 - 154 pages paperback. Classic fictional portrayal of the head to head poker game between "The Kid" and "Lancey Hodges" immortalised in the Pual Newman - Edward G Robinson film.

POKER: HOLD'EM - Andy Nelson - £6-95 - 74 pages paperback. Useful guide to inceasingly popular poker variant covering position, reading the opponents, studying the flop, raising, knowing when to get out, know how to apply the odds, keeping records.